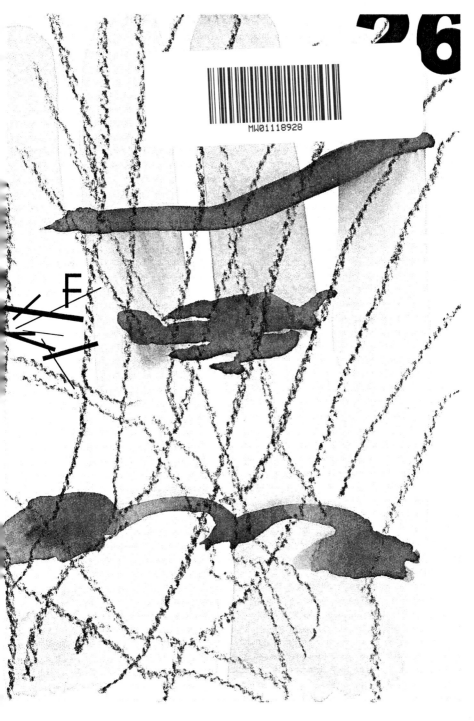

26

a b c d e ░ g h i j k l m n o p q r s t u v w x y z

A journal of poetry and poetics

SAN FRANCISCO BAY AREA ° 2007

Editors: Avery E. D. Burns, Brian Strang
Intern: Andrew Kenower
Cover art: Norma Cole
Cover design and logo: Jacek Ostoya
Interior design and typesetting: Jaime Robles

ISBN 1-889098-10-8

Web Address: www.26magazine.com
Send submissions to **26**, P.O. Box 4450, Saint Mary's College, Moraga, CA
94575-4730. We read submissions from June 1– August 31. Notification
occurs in September. All submissions should be accompanied by a SASE. We
do not accept electronic submissions. We do not accept simultaneous submissions.

Subscriptions: $20 for two-year subscription; tax-deductible lifetime
subscription $260. All additional contributions are deeply appreciated and
tax-deductible. $12 individual issues. Individual and back issues are also
available through Small Press Distribution.

SAINT MARY'S COLLEGE
of California

26 is affiliated with the Saint Mary's
College MFA Program in Creative Writing.
For more information about the program contact
Christopher Sindt at 925-631-4088.

We would also like to thank Chris Sindt for his
invaluable support.

Contents

magining form

This year, 2006, has brought big changes to 26. Co-founding editors, Rusty Morrison, Joseph Noble and Elizabeth Robinson have moved on to other projects. The remaining editors thank them for their hard work and vision in making this magazine a success. Their absence brings change; this cannot be the same magazine without them. What direction it will take in the future we can only imagine and imagine it we must because we have no other or better tool for grappling with the unknown.

During a talk in June, physicist Stephen Hawking advocated migration away from the earth, announcing that "Life on earth is at an ever-increasing risk of being wiped out by a disaster, such as sudden global warming, nuclear war, a genetically engineered virus, or other dangers we have not yet thought of."

Other dangers we have not yet thought of? This inelegant phrase from a brilliant mind strikes hard because it invites us to conjure the worst from the unknown—imagination of annihilation. Destruction lies beyond the limits of our knowledge and capability to grasp what we have no way of imagining. But, whether Hawking intended it or not, there is an implicit promise here as well. If we cannot imagine the future accurately, could it be that unforeseeable events, the unimaginable, might offer salvation as well? Certainly history is full of examples of previously unimaginable events unfolding seemingly without precedent.

Sufis see imagination as an intermediary, a sort of connection, between the human and divine. *In Sufism and Surrealism* the Lebanese poet Adonis says "Between the known and unknown worlds lies what Ibn 'Arabi calls barzakh (the intermediate world)." This world, according to Adonis is "the site in which things are transformed, i.e. the site of images and revelations." And, according to Adonis, Ibn 'Arabi believes that "imagination is the largest of beings and the most perfect of created things, although it is in constant motion, existing-non-existing, known-unknown, negative-positive at the same time." Seen this way, Hawking's warnings could also be asking us to delve into an intermediate zone full of both risk and promise.

The outer boundary of knowledge has always proven irre-sistible, and we have sought to imagine it in order to achieve it. Hera-clitus pointed to the ineffable nature of wisdom:

> Of all the words yet spoke,
> none comes quite as far as wisdom,
> which is the action of the mind
> beyond all things that may be said.

And he claimed that Logos was divine:

> Wisdom is the oneness
> of mind that guides
> and permeates all things.

(tr. Haxton)

If wisdom is both ineffable and absolute, it is no great stretch to understand imagination as a speculative form of wisdom, a link to something beyond what may be said. For the Sufi, Adonis claims, imag-ination is elevating, the means to achieve an elevated or divine state:

Imagination does not aim to persuade but rather to create the marvelous and the sweet; it does not aim to produce mere curiosities, but rather to enrich the sensitivity and expand the consciousness, so that the reader will feel that everything before him [sic] is beginning again and is taking on a new meaning.

History is replete with examples of humankind's ability to imagine the worst for each other, so Adonis' assertion that it leads only to the "marvelous and sweet" is shaky at best. Imagination itself doesn't aim at all, is neither purely malevolent nor beneficent and has no will and does not reason or make judgments. But it does enrich and embellish (for better and worse). And the loss of it inspires dread; Beckett titled his chilling vignette of a white static eternity "Imagination Dead Imagine." It is a world of the worst kind of paralysis, an entombed and embalmed state, utterly reductive, without a trace of hope or possibility.

But imagination is what allows Beckett to conjure this fear and so another formula might take its place beside Beckett's title: "Image begins imagination." Or is it "Imagination begins image?" In "Byzantium" Yeats recognizes the generative and visionary power of the image: "Those images that yet/Fresh images beget." And languages are full of words that speak to the reciprocal and relative relationship between the image and understanding: "seer," "foresight," "viewpoint." In this sense being able to "see," or imagine, is to access to an intermediary realm between contrasting terms, between the human and divine (for the Sufi and others) or between different points of view. It allows for the ability to empathize: "I see what you mean." Adonis points to the potential of this intermediary realm:

The image makes possible the concrete translation of reality. It allows one to go beyond the power of reason and it gives form to an individual perception of the world. It brings together two ways of perceiving the world, without elevating one over the other.

It is impossible to adequately define the relationship between the serial or sequence poem and the imagination because there is no consensus about what this form means or of what it is capable; so much has been written about it and there are unique poetics for each poet and poem: "Each lyric sequence creates its own music. Each lyric sequence creates its own world(s)," writes Joseph Lease.

The serial poem is also a specific form closely associated with a specific school of poetry, namely that of Spicer, Duncan, Blaser, et al., and therefore has a specific poetic history, one that has had a great deal of influence on poets writing today. The shape of this issue, was, in fact, determined by the kind of work we received, evidence perhaps of this influence. And Tom Orange sees the serial poem not as a historical form but as one that remains alive and full of potential:

> Serial form strikes me today as the form of choice for many poets working in alternative, avant-garde, experimental, innovative or non-mainstream traditions. Immanently versatile, serial form enables a shaping and ordering of materials into a product that can be open-ended or finite, sustained or discontinuous, procedural or intentional, or any combination or range therein. Inherently non-hierarchical, serial form rejects notions of the masterwork that underpin both the individual poem (as a discrete entity collected into a sequence or book) and the modern-day epic or longpoem. Whereas these latter forms are marked by ambition, serial form is decidedly modest in scope and scale.

The modesty inherent in the serial form seems to arise from an awareness of the enormity of the task facing the poet writing in a form that doubts its own efficacy. Devon Wootten claims that "the serial poem is an utterance in crisis. It teeters between faith and despair. It labors. It fails but cannot resolve itself to failure. It reiterates. It stumbles. It staggers forward. " It stumbles forward into what cannot be imagined, and for this it must contain an incomplete quality, a lack of certitude or ultimate definition.

But while the effectiveness of the form may be in doubt, it is clear that many of the poets within this issue have pointed to the incomplete nature of the form as an attempt to connect with, to imagine, the ineffable (or the "void"): "The serial poem is a gesture toward wholeness rather than an assertion thereof. The serial poem acknowledges the void and thereby engages it. It cries, "Some progress must be made!" while at the same time asking, "Can any progress be made?," " writes Wootten. Here is an uncertain gesture toward the intermediary zone, beyond what might be said with certainty.

This gesture takes on (counter) magical potential for Elise Ficarra who describes *Counterspell* as a pressurized cube, one she wants to crack. Compression becomes a generative tool to unlock and activate imagination, to dispel the passive and hypnotized state of enchantment:

> I was thinking about the forces that hold us in enchantment and wanting to pressurize that cube to find the cracks in the structure where things break-down and something happens inside the cube that exceeds the cube and breaks the spell, constituting a new body, which is among other things, the body of the audience receiving the work.

The poem becomes a vehicle, a talisman, for physical transformation, both on the page and in the mind of the reader/audience and, perhaps, poet. In this conception of the serial or sequential work, we return to Sufism's desire: to move beyond what is known, to an intermediary zone where everything is beginning anew.

RAE ARMANTROUT

What We Mean

Oh Princess,
you apple-core afloat

in coke
in a Styrofoam cup,
on an end-table,

you dust, glass, book, crock, thorn, moon.

Oh Beauty who fell asleep
on your birthday,

we swipe at you.

*

How are we defining "dream?"

An exaggerated sense

of the relevance
of these details,

of "facts"
as presented?

A peculiar
reluctance to ask

presented by whom,
and in what space?

*

By space we mean
the collapsible

whirligig
of attention,

the figuring and
reconfiguring

of charges

among orbits
                (obits)

that has taken forever

Own

Woman in a room near mine moans, "I'm dying. I want to be fine. It's my body!
"Don't let me! Don't touch me!"

*

By definition,
I'm the blip
floating across my own
" field of vision."

*

On closed eyes I see the spartan wall of the ICU
covered in a scrambled hodge-podge of sticky notes,
crossing one another at all angles,
illegibly written over, snippets of reference,
madly irrelevant.

*

 Symbolism as the party face of paranoia.

Chorus of expert voices beyond my door, forever dissecting my case.

"But the part is sick
of representing the whole."

*

"We will prevail,"
says the leader on multiple
screens. The words
are empty, but he's there
 inside the lie
everyone believes—
that nothing
will really change. He's become pure
being, insisting
only on insistence.

*

A crowd (scene) of cells, growing wildly,
by random access to stock types,
(Play any role you like and go on
forever. Who is speaking?)
Able to draw blood vessels to itself
by emitting a mock distress call.

*

From deep time,
patterns
on my grandmother's crockery
rise
to cover my closed eyelids,
lumpy fruits and flowers, brown
against a cream background.

*

Dream that Aaron is telling friends to be quiet because he's listening to
a rumble,
a white noise voice from his own intestines which he believes
is telling him how to save me. "SHH!" he says to anyone who speaks.

KATE COLBY

The Flood
from **"A Banner Year"**

Moved   making site   (un)
seen   and only so by saying,
the grounds for the acreage;
a mirage imagined as cast, if only
in plaster reproductions, waxworks
and knock-offs of famous figurines.

If not tantamount, then dead
ringer candy that tastes exactly like
its flavor is the end-all object
of her world-class habitation

      (the world being un-invented,
      re-cast to resemble a medicine ball
      as it lately equivocates Chinatown.
      Grandfather worked with a set as a means
      of regaining dexterity after a stroke.
      Here, it's a world nested next to itself
      in a cheap silk box and a dull
      ringing, removed from the Ming, then itself,
      en masse, many times repurposed
      as degrees of evidence of travel,
      and herein also as a state:)

having it made.

A retaining wall forms
rings built bucking trends
and provisional returns
always to where it left off
its off-putting case of countless
stairs of no dependable provenance
but allusion

a widow's walk

determined

to overlook
          the sense of not seeing
          hands drawing hands
          weaving cords of concentrics
          that never cross, (supposing)
          this sort of illusion as optical
          preference

having no bearing   a Pre-Raphaelite
                                    hanging in the anteroom
Compliant lighting recessed
in effect, *trompe l'oeil* tiers
made ready by LASIK,
pipes banging
          (who goes there?)
water hammers and canned
arrangements, stringy canons
wind upward with modular
equipment of upmarket value:
delicate vapors, mustard, plasters,
and a sparse and tonic-y comb-over.

Hairline cracks spread settling
studs and flagstones, floorboards
scatter light by way of slats, cast
tinny sounds of tacks in exaction,
alloyed, daft and dull.

    coffers nested
    inside coffers

a stack
of battered

portmanteaux   her empty
                    portable museum

(The ante is the upshot)
Her weakness is for nesting
keepsakes in Bakelite,
the utmost in tractable laminates, practical
hot and cold in open taps and personal
effects of scented products

affecting nature
naturata and pro-
rated as identical,
easy, protracted
installments

       buying securities
       on margin

       a definition
       of leverage

       the trunks contain
       the tokens of severance

The value is in sticker shock
affixed to lilies gilded
with traceless cultivation

drawn   water

curtains   thread

bare & worn   as gold-

braided   hardware   (breath)

drawing   room

> in ready-made obsolescence
> and comes with a free patina
> of limitation   blue as Jodhpur

(draw back: the cellar
walls sweat and run, pool
beneath pallets of expired vintage.)

(In Jodhpur there are three given reasons
for which the city walls are painted blue.
Depends on who you ask. Nobody
remembers. Here, the walls are also blue,
blue as Jodhpur.)

Precipitate clouds gather
a program of copper pots, reflected
bugging Breton omelets
(crept behind the drywall—)

On a cliff outside the walls of Saint-Malo,
Chateaubriand is interred with broken waves
and the creeping of the groundcover.

true blue and
verdigris

This is the land
that grows
around me.

To the wine, preferring
(incongruous) output of
Trappists, hearts of organ-
isms that grow in heads

And shapes come to look
like the shapes
they once stood for.

No sleep is never enough.

Dimpled glass on the nightstand
        sidelong
            you should be in pictures

dividing till there's no difference

there are not books   enough
the last word   still
in the works   not
with   standing
room   enough

    While she sleeps
    sidereal sucking
    mechanisms
    parsed into categories
    of survivability

the air around her breathes   if she could only lie
still

TOM ORANGE

from **25 Poems**

come out of
dust, you misguided
sentience: we go
to the seer
out of fierce hurt
or posthumous
conjecture, victims
tuned utterly
to the bones
of cryogenic
dreams no less
than those who
bid over my
wept one

love of something
higher and they
are of earth
in august and
pain has ground
them down to
where they have
fled—ornaments
a sort of blunt
torture that rages
upon any of
the syllables
they come now
only to outlive

checkmate is double
blind if half the
world is earth and
half is blood:
to the beautiful
trouble of outdoors
ocean forever offers
a foreign day that
trembles with you
as you fall into
that night so wild
thrashing at the
starcolors a painter
might find to give

with my deaths
forever rambling
to contrive each
other that you
could enter
there and clasp
far more than
float—that you
could still soar
through the strange
surge like a noon
sun wagering
a wilderness
on its seasons

first a snowfall of
sudden glass comes
then we skip another
eternity etched and
singing the shattered
scroll on which
it is written—
together with the
beautiful trouble
that befalls all it
lies ever tenuous
on the ordinary
heather repenting
those citizens lost

unknown fled and
always flown the
thousands through
gate of day, unheard
eyes made from
the nest you feel
in—again you
breathed the
stars angels
lacquered and
loved honing out
of loyalty for
summer guests
dear to you

loving you paler
ultimately in all
of what we want
to pillow through,
the rivers and weeds
we till: hand me
that little silence
there and look
through to some
long lineage of
pleasures, the
palpitating heads
and breathing hands
we would eat from

folly the frozen
populace in a basement
of silence—only
arms and stone he
sees her question
now for every-
thing and children
everywhere in
the stench of
false wages—
night is a use
ago, a green pit
the doubtful nymph
eyes with splinters

mine age has
wrought a lovely
kiss to light a
common night
and now composure
holds the storm
deserted into white—
beyond loud chasms
looking chasing
never to behold
what common
snares of memory
have wanted
to be sold

the room might
not desire an
answer tonight, the
dusk in sight
you faked and
universal death
that slows me
like grass—
with the frozen
plucking of it some
use there serenely
to avert what
laughs near darkness
through you

thousands tread
through the tunnel
of halfsound, desire
left not far afield
after cheerfulness
and willows, when
the pure green says
nothing—light is
forever corrugated
and shuts the
roar while you
fall always in
all then drop
and come

celebrate with me
the hour of our
lie, an other
damned to share
this curse like
three spirits strangely
moulded in the
stops of dark stars—
look there now
where a word is
born over in magic
death moments, its
readership a sky
of choral water

thought is mad
with the silence
of its ancestors
while we double
our fake truths
for want of art—
unmoor your
moment from time,
take and grow
your letters flashing
in the marine sun
from that which
i happily place
their body upon

sing through snow
between the unfathom-
able learned of
it and myself
though both growing
and dying are
long—spare
now the hand and
fervent talk humming
and flowing on
here where we
imagine everything
to exist not frozen
but in blindfold

clean came her
believing from the
agony of chains
a sweet woven
heaven beckoning
each away from the
shaken blue stream-
side—within these
walls of sunlit
sense go each
life to lose the
seen and said on
the fire of every
gentle hour after

mine the entangled
in wonder and
wither—silver
knees that cut
and tear your
blame they
refuse to show
what color
two rivers have
in common with
sky when spirit
has mirrored
them in its own
hair and arms

that you sound
the buried hours of
thick jade, it leans
out full into us and
feels like conversation,
lightning movement
loosened from its
shell to guard down
the icey tide of
sweet idle weeping—
it eases us now from
the stormy white
having spent its little
elegaic brilliance

MARY BURGER

I Like Purple

for Iris Vitiello, age almost 6

"I like purple, " she says. "I don't know why."

She tapes plastic farm animals to a piece of cardboard and calls it a farm. She has colored the cardboard green. We accept her premise.

It wasn't so hard to understand what we'd done—
create a work in which "being" was always in question—
but the existence of the work defied understanding.

A study on narrative positivism—*the novel represents public and private space, violence represents subconscious urges*—cannot account for it.

Walk me through the body.

That everything be a playlet—the accordion-playing rabbit, the finely-detailed plastic hippo ("West Germany"), the fish vase with the round hole eye and the open mouth, the Indonesian shadow puppet, all enact a drama on the dining room table—and we keep going, as if we knew their parts and could play them.

The truth came out: I did not know how to read.

An ego gets formed, and a vocabulary, which may at first seem easy, even trite, may seem to determine specific ideas, may seem to prevent the transformation of an embroidered peasant shawl into a wriggling hallucination—girls lined up, one row above another, as if in the corridors of a cell block, a bar or scarf floating across their middle, and below the heads of the next row, the bars moved and danced with the girls, and it seemed the whole system might split, but it didn't.

from "The Man Without Stumps, Part I"

This gaseous gray cloud may be just what happens when blood is not able to mix with water.

_____

I started too hard, my hands came right off, splintery white bone at the ends of my wrists, red-spattered whisk brooms.

_____

The fibers pull apart at the last possible moment, the white tissue dissolves to reveal pale blue sky. The tissue has the rubbery consistency of cartilage, a gelatinous, non-fibrous solid.

_____

The man without stumps lolls his head from side to side.

_____

Even nature can be overcome. Even death. Just ask the man in the yellow jersey. He is like a boy today.

_____

The man without stumps saved a life once in World War II, pulled another man to safety when their ship went down, put the rope of the life raft in his teeth and swam several miles to shore.

Even nature can be used to master itself. Just ask the man in the yellow jersey. He is made of tungsten steel. His tight clothes are one with his body.

The man in the yellow jersey has done his best today. He has triumphed over competition, he has ridden every hill faster than every other man. He has had the simple triumphs of a boy.

He was a companion while I steered myself out of the harbor. He thought that he would come along, but he got scared by the full moon on open water and waded back. The water was up to his chest the whole time, walking five hundred feet was like walking five miles, his feet sank into the slippery sand and had no traction, he pushed against the muck with each foot and went nowhere, really he had to thrust each leg forward and pull with both arms, it was like swimming but it was harder, to try to push against a surface when really one was moving—

The man without stumps drools on himself.

A feel for the water, that's what swimmers call it, knowing by feel how to adjust to the pressure and force of the fluid, to make one's stroke the most efficient.

The man without stumps goes careening down the hill. He can't stop but he's not worried. He knows he's too strong to break. A few bruises will liven him up, remind him of the boundaries between him and the outside world. He likes playing through the pain, he likes feeling brave enough to take the risk.

He bumps and bounces along the rocks piled at the bottom. He comes to a stop, wedged in a crevice, one wheel spinning in a quiet whir, calling attention in its soft way after the rumble and crashing of the way down.

We are always raising tents, laying the poles on the ground in the radiating pattern, spreading the canvas out flat to the edges and attaching it to the poles, heaving the poles up in a great coordinated effort to raise the roof. Small haze-covered sky, no light breaks in except through the cracks in the fabric walls. Always at the fulcrum of the lisft, there is a chance someone will give out. One pole will swerve wildly, others will waver, and suddenly the whole sailing sky will lurch to one side and collapse, entangling the pole-raisers in white fabric too opaque to see through and too engulfing to throw off. There is cursing, some laughing, some "oh well, here we are again," some resolve, some get-up-and-go. There is, eventually, some success, either that or the era passes, the time for tents ends, there is a last time that the tent is raised, thought nobody may know it's the last time as it's happening, they may not know until it's over.

ABDELKRIM TABAL translated from Arabic by Wendy Walker and Rabia Zabkh

Truth

A coach

bowls along backwards, with us inside it

and the demented coachman

all alone

bowls along in front

who himself reports this hallucination

so you'd better believe him

A Mirror

A reflection of mountains

in a lark's voice

he who lofts the sea

above the clouds

A Gazelle

Sir

don't take the path

used by

the jackal   and his mates

by the prince   and his minions

they are of one kind

all breakfast on blood

then throw back the shutters

A Beginning

The rain

may give me wings

to flow through the body of grass

till I observe

how water turns green

without a brush

searching whiteness

Dear Sir

It doesn't preoccupy me

what is said   and what isn't said

who forges the swords

and who embroiders the shawl

and who comes to the throne

and who ascends a bier

and who's in a cage

and who's in a radiant forest

These things don't preoccupy me

but a rhyme

in a celebration

of this land

this sky

Martyrdom

You, the swimmer

in a droplet

let yourself drown

till you see

the sun of love

Guarded

They applied their seals

to the door

and they withdrew

to a blind corridor

inside me

A Mask

The mark

of horses' hooves

in the gem

of your gold ring

So how will you teach us

the lives of the prophets?

Gallantry

A cactus

stamps a dwelling

on the sand's fire

may lodge a rabbit

lost

in the desert

JULIET PATTERSON

Approaching Scenic View

.

Toward a flower-
ing I came

lowly lupine raised
wrist

a loop of memory & its variable
eye

white pine

the deer coming closer

Out of she
to you

How many sights
circle

How many sights
position against

the ear of my ear & the ghost
of the ear

Sumac, Winter Rain

Seeded, a 'somewhere' pulled
the veins

net flow across ribs studded with berries
in the curved harbor

the letters of the words of our legs and arms
thin, pointed

each branch illustrating morning's beautiful profusion
waking a lamp, a scratch, a hole

the flat & empty landscape
on the far side

of the lake
where morning's ice lacquers that color

a wrist hoisted its ankles after
to forget the bombing

North Central Entreaty

Dispensed against the retina
into the novice spread of horse-
nettle

a caterpillar settles near the open door

locked on infinite regress

becomes the familiar return
of images

like water over
terrain: a day slips

where we stand in a stranger's field
beyond pardon

small teeth are set deep

with the sifting noise of a wrist
on paper

truth this inhuman fixing & all the earth
a lens

lipped apex

distillate & vapor

lines 1-3 adapted from Forrest Gander

LAURA MORIARTY

A Tonalist War

And why are we fighting, he asked. Because we want the world, in
which our literature belongs, to be freed of disfigurement.

—Peter Weiss, *Aesthetics of Resistance*

But who is out there
Birding the sun?

And what is left?
A long morning followed

By a long night
The linear battlefield of yesterday

A list of the dead vexes
The president's vacation

Like meteorology he is in the prediction business
But when did you realize you could be a lucid dreamer?

The skin white as marble
Or the marbleized sky means

Rain sometimes
A catastrophe or no rain

Or the earth is the weather
History is the same

When a war is fought between Turkey and Russia, France enters and England, calling it the Crimean War. Until recently, it was known as history's most unnecessary war. The generals who were to fight the Civil War in the US visited the Crimea to learn about the modern battlefield. Marx reported on it for the Times. Marbles were being excavated then in Turkey, according to Peter Weiss, but their removal was not affected by the war.

> After the war the Arts and Crafts movement
> Begins in England and finds an ideal home
>
> In California's *Philosopolis*
> As William and Lucia Matthews
>
> Called their magazine
> Or later in *Semina*, a California
>
> Or two ago, Wallace Berman
> Replaces paradise with itself

A cataclysm of natural and historical forces occurs. We don't feel it until we do. One by one our lives are changed or saved or lost. Catastrophes increase in frequency until there is one every day and then one every hour. "Are you prepared for disaster?" the supermarket loudspeaker asks when I am in San Diego. The firestorm season comes and the border burns. No one is ready when something burns.

> When the weather kills
> We are reminded by death
>
> That death is natural
> Displacement everyday

Anguish ordinary and
Inevitable the word

Compassion comes up
Capacity also

Many writers are cultural workers. Others work for causes as
fundraisers or administrators. Others for businesses or institutions
that provide a variety of products, as books, that can be used to resist
the powers that, however, ultimately control the businesses in question, if not the products themselves. Who has this control? How can it
be demonstrated? Or can we stipulate that the control exists and that
it is inimical to anyone whose class affiliation is lower than upper? Do
we think that these activities matter because someone, somewhere
(perhaps it is ourselves) can get access to something that would otherwise remain hidden or invisible? Tell a story here. Show that the work
of making the invisible visible is endless, that a new version is constantly required.

Can you stray from your class?
Or does language itself determine

Your intentions. What are
Your intentions?

Does the fact that *The Daily Compromise*
Was founded in 2000 mean

That nothing can be done?
I can prove the opposite proposition

With any of your lines

"Working notes handed out." [Taylor Brady]

"Gutenberg is watching" [Alan Halsey]
"A shred of cloud totally profiling
bruise." [Alli Warren]

"Your mistrust, fellow citizens, is natural." [Brent Cunningham]

Reaching for the books that are to hand
You find a familiar lexicon but belief

Where do you find that?
Is the bruise visible?

Is it legible? They meet in a room to discuss art while the war
goes on. Some people die every day. There are automated phone calls.
They sound real. Art is the thing they do. The people in this room.
Glamour means everything to them and they would die, glamorously,
to bring about what they felt was fundamental change. Others quietly
persist. Still others, not in the room, feel that if they can convince us
that people, enemies of freedom, also not in the room, are trying to
kill us, we will allow them to do anything. Let's call them the government. These would-be killers identify the US with the government.
They say there is no difference between us and it. Thinking of them
with compassion is not the same as doing nothing.

The silence of the afternoon air
In this grove is expensive

However you look at it you
Don't usually see it from the chair

At your desk where the question is
Can you comprehend

The whole set-up while you are
Implicated in its outcome?

The real weather is the war
We are all in

We can't stop them
As in arrest is to cause

To rest but there is no
Time for that we say stop

But should we simply
Stop having begun?

When will it be time to go, if not now?
The religious people will take over

As they have done here
Making it illegal not to answer

About yourself under
The Patriot Act even if

As a patriot you consider it
Your duty not to answer

The Dalai Lama speaks about compassion. He says it's too early to decide about the war. What is he thinking? Perhaps about the loss of his country to the invasion by China. The world let it happen.

We are the world. The statues were broken. The marble ground down like bones.

Deadly asymmetrical events
Precede visits by uniformed

Messengers dreaded
By those who wait

Those who go don't
Want to go but are

Overtaken by events
And the consequences of not

Going so they go
Fathers and or gang members

According to Sean Labrador
Whose father as mine

Went to war
But what are we doing now?

What is the genre of this activity? Is it a street fight, a humanitarian rescue, a diplomatic mission or all three simultaneously and by turns. Unpredictable and sudden, things change from one to the other. The term Three Block Warfare can refer to these actions or to the three city blocks in which they often occur. Network Centric Warfare is another term, meaning the use of knowledge processing in battle as well as the synchronizing and swarming of small groups in an unstable environment of intense conflict. Decisions are made there by individuals whose training is brief, whose knowledge is limited and whose central motive is to stay out of the line of fire.

> By means of fire
> For which there are special names
>
> At different times "We don't do a lot of
> Hearts and minds here it's irrelevant
>
> Amateurs talk about theory
> Professionals about logistics

How to get it done? As in any job, it's the same thing over and over. How to move things from here to there. Wait for the election to fight the battle. Stuff happens. My enemy's enemies are my friends. Religious fundamentalists in cahoots with each other from the US and Iran. This is what Iraqis believe according to the Baghdad Burning blogger. What does she know?

> White phosphorus is Whiskey Pete
> Made from pee by alchemists
>
> In the 17th century "It was
> 17th century tactics" a soldier says
>
> Of Fallujah "It's under siege"
> As fury fantisizes or vigilance resolves
>
> Marines, Iraqi security and commandos
> Begin "debriding Fallujah of it guerillas"
>
> According to Time
> It is called the cold light

It burns through the person leaving the clothes intact. It is not cold. They were seeking the philosopher's stone. It is conventional to burn people during a war. They always mention the bones. It burns to the bones.

Lies, fire, things that explode
Deployed conventionally

Poetic as weapon
"against logical analysis" [Alan Halsey]

Synthesizes "sense, shape & sound" so that the words are the event and the event is not explicable and can't be paraphrased. Nothing is the same. History is yesterday.

Standing there lost in memory I started to hear the skeletal scrape of leaves bouncing along the driveway. For a second I caught a familiar scent on the wind, the smoky tang of seasoned wood crackling on a fire. That phantom smell was enough to soften the cold lines of the forward operating base, and the next breath I took pushed me even farther into memory. For a few minutes … I was home. I could see the flickering incandescence of a fireplace dance on my wife's face. I could hear her voice, as pure as claret and as bright as the searing embers in the fire. I don't know how long I remained absorbed in thought—dreams and memories follow their own meandering path through time. Eventually I heard the rooftop door groan heavily on its dried hinges, the tortured sound pulling me back across the long miles. Back across the oceans of sand, and it scattered islands of pain and strife. Back across the fierce shoals of vehicles and weapons that ring our encampment. Until I was once again standing on an ugly roof. In Baghdad. Alone.
[Danjel Bout, 365 and a Wakeup, blog]

The afternoon panic is silent, is the poem
"More accurate than any report"?

What is the worst you have seen?
He asks his father on the way to Iraq

There is a huge book called *The Torture Papers*
He is a plastic surgeon

I can't repeat the story, he says
It dreams about the war

THOMAS A. CLARK

sunshine its climate
openness its aspect
detail its pleasure

not a stranger in the glen
without a rumour on the breeze
not a stray sheep on the hill
without word of it

a path through the gold
of bird's foot trefoil
turning by the pink
of thrift or campion

where it turns
in the long grasses
you are there
ahead of yourself
drawn forward
by implication
away from yourself

thrift, campion
bird's foot trefoil
you are coloured
by events

green islands
on blue seas
blue lochans
on green islands

drifting between
green islands
a red boat
on blue water

sit down on the rocks
impatience exhausted
thyme, thrift and clover
where the space is wide
hours should be wasted
thyme, thrift and clover

between sea and sky
drifts of bugloss
a blue butterfly
lifting from the lyme grass

cormorant and herring gull
orpine and clover
sorrel and sea kale
redshank and plover

spray-washed
wind-dried
sheep-bitten
sand-blasted

the little ringed plover
with its broken wing
the brittle insistences
of dunlin and sanderling

a wide stretch of sand

you walk out
into space
as to
an appointment

with so much
space around you
intention
drops from you

here is where
forward momentum
runs out in
pure extension

no longer
ahead of yourself
in imagination
or behind yourself
pushing forward

you walk
above yourself
space spreading round you
the sand
bearing your weight

leaving everything
which is not itself
outside itself

a black stone

for as far as you can go
over the machair
there is only surface

it is a plane
of appearance where nothing
is deferred

lacking in depth
you walk on the richly
embroidered surface

heard but not seen
the corncrake in the grasses
steps through fragrance

shy of exposure
seeking the shelter
of complexity and fragrance

asphodel, milkwort
eyebright, ling
the lovely particulars
brighter than their names

through crushed water-mint
through particulars you come
to a green boat moored
beside purple vetch

the blue butterfly's
moment on the purple
thistle flower
is indolent

idly its hoarded
blue is unfolded
onto difference
then folded again

turn back from the sea
from margins and limits

behind yellow dune and grey dune
beyond the old hay meadows
follow your inclination
a drift of thistledown

at leisure a shape
lifts from rock and flaps
out over wastes
a few wing beats
taking it far

ANNE WALDMAN

Book of Light: Secrets of the Ambulatories

She's up observing the moon set, and had been studying Robert Smith-
son & Mel Bochner's The Domain Of The Great Bear where the plan-
etarium becomes the same size as the universe.And notes the Secrets of
The Ambulatories and the phrase "Sundial Motto "I mark only the
sunny hours". How to calibrate her time, urgent now, toward greater
purpose.The notion of "exposure" haunts her investigations. About
4.600 million years ago, the earth mass was already in circumstances
that were to suitable for the emergence of life. It was near the sun. By
astronomical reckoning the sun has a lifetime of ten billion years. We
homo sapiens will reach extinction with or without a nuclear war. We
may like ichthyosaurs, seed ferns and australopithecines leave without
an heir or we might like choanomastigotes and Homo erectus evolve
into distinct new species. How will we mutate without light? And back
in small-time-mind fifty years from nows be confined in the dark cor-
ners of our dwellings unable to brave the heat of the sun between the
hours of noon and one p.m. Tundra of Siberia by some accounts
"methane bubbled up so steadily that puddles of standing water
wouldn't freeze even in the depths of a Russian winter".

  keep open your daily book of light,
as you might say book of "days"
or "nights:
book of "hours" book of "sighs"
  book of receptacles
 or phantasms resound
    of optical illusions in light

keep your raconteur-motif going:
in or about or on in depth of light

Scheherazade on a whim...
   command the world spin one more time
every facet informing every other global twist

tiny crystal integuments
 or a witch's brew, a chant within which
   we state with perfect authority
"the moon is a flame"

whatever the Ayatollah might say to the contrary
& however you regard the silk trade of Thailand
or whoever you rate as "enemy"

the flame is still munificent in your eye

does the eye alight on the bird with impunity?
does the eye wait in predatory ambush?
can you resolve temporality this one last time?

(a mind may be soothed by its own narration)

(moon going down)

or should we just all go home now?

but you retain without hesitation
 a flawless sea-faring mentality
Ecrasez l'infame! we wrote on the sign
   for the DC confrontation, red-lettered

restless, rocked by waves, who gets or gets not to vote?
woman of swabbed decks, of sails, of tempests
looking up at the clear sky (storm passed now,
    thunder gone down)
with a sailor's delight one more time
waiting in line yea or nay, ahoy

does the eye jump to attention?
does the eye turn up the volume?
how much light in your atmosphere
will the treachery of governance be exposed?

keep the same book open—gaining ground now—
    for rapture's sake,
    a magic lantern in mythical time
as if metaphor or philology
disarms your witness—who is it?
    & of from planet does she come

& what got
 ruptured— & in whose arms
& will the angry citizens do no harm?
hold that image now—give it double exposure

red evokes a revolt in me
    and escapes my text...

black cries out for vengeance...

the white of the photo...deadly phosphorus...
    invades the page

is it safe?

is it marketable?

   in and outside of itself and of its
relationship to you, the dreamer in light—

the window
   holds

 such refractions now

the text summons light of sex, a fleshly hold,
summons the riot police who quell light of courage
to challenge "we had to come here"
30.000 policemen surround the building
of those exposing criminals to light
the one responsible for keeping track of light you are
and of things responsive to light that could posit symmetrically
change the frequency of how to speak of it: struggle for
fair trade, compassion in and out of focus, put a
spotlight on Mozambique, not destroy a livelihood
put the bodies against the barricades, develop my country
with perspicacity, let me sleep, body weary when the sun goes down...

freedom of speech! take care for the animal kingdom!
revive endangered plants! summon endangered languages!
and make clear to light its purpose in being that which exposures
      and
notice how it will move,
shift,
   shine in your environs if you only behave

shine in your emotions

reflects off all your shiny passable things
—your overt ones—
all the gloss of surface upon them
 lamp vase table book

and wants to have you
     take notes on its qualities &
offer praise:
how you might through observing light
become light's double
light's doppelganger
light's trader
lights' traitor
lights lover
beholden to a mistress light

how you
  might inhabit a particular person
    through light
seen in hazel eye, glint of tooth,
polish of nail, angle where hair's sheen
  might break a heart, entangled bodies
    or ankle flash its reward in running
how is it to be human under such light?
who turned it on? or afternoon ablution
  shimmering by the door
    object situation   support to
      keep life going
(altars go high for the trance-stone)
how does it exist in words in images

in "reportorial" in "untarnished" in "toadstone"
in "striated" in "sequin"
what is the most desirous tableau?
from what inscrutable angle
did "this was a rock" come?
or "this was a glass"
or this was an object of torture
was this someone you cared for?
this was a child
this was the *auto-da-fe* you were waiting for
this was a replicate of the earlier light-rail
this took place
    at a particular
time of day when you were desired and loved

    that brought the ravishing shadows on bodies,
  on objects and the
notion of
    Inside versus Outside light
  as in the Cretaceous when dinosaurs went extinct

66 millions years ago

what destructive planetoid entered from "outer space"
hit the planet hard causing a world-wide blackout?
who was watching?

write a little
    speech about oracular Light
  that might be interjected into a script
    write some sentences, or a list
  from the point of view
      of light

    meager graffiti
        what are its glowing properties?
notice
text
still talks
get over
get out
Jacques Rivette's Joan the Maid
  burns with her paper hat on: *heretique*
& what were the crimes?

  warned in the forewarned repository
    not to heed voices

Il supplizio dell'ebreo

pragmatism first
then let me represent your body with
words: "woman", "man",all the
conventionalized signs
"straight", "gay", "diverse"
but "in between" too
mute chambers squawk
for recognition
Hindu goddess?
scarf of Islam?
daughter of Rebeccah?
opaque Quatro Century madonna?
Dakini on a spree?
Goddess Durga churning the world in her maw?
Life is possible, she says, with my body
which is woman all the way down
which is imagination and desire

all the way up towards "heaven"
(palace keeps Byzantine weirdness)
(an aligned notice for goblets)
pleated transparencies, twinkle of an eye
gesture, plea, shock, surprise
in a topsy-turvy world beyond gender:
the light is the mask
the light is the musk
the light is the corner
the light is the book
the pillow is the desk
the foot is the plinth
the wall is the story
the mirror is the future
the hand is a ghost
the flame is the consort
the face is the past
the face is the gem
the machine is the conduit
the night is the telegram
the closet is the mannerism
the brow is the labor
the sweat is the mistress
the tree is the repository
its aspen leave turn yellow
the tray is the mesa
the glass is the thirst
the mountain is the curse
the mountain is the guest
the road is the rational
her language is strange
her language desires interpretation
the forest is the saint

the alluvials let go
the jungle is underneath
civilization is laceration
the hurricane is relentless
the masters are exposed
the front is a sham
the dice are repetitive
the draw is the draw
the throw is the queen
the woman looks down
the clock trembles
the water is dangerous
the shutter responds
the shutter speeds up
the hand resists the mother
the tide shifts
the creatures crawl back under the roof
the shell is the galaxy
the shell is the shelter
the galaxy is armored
the monolith is in place
the ruler is the tinderbox
the fire is the stair
the ladder is the question
war will never happen
the arm is the stranger
the mouth is the mystery
the elbow is the shelter
the tooth is the machine
the tongue is the text
the ear is the world
the nipple is the cause
the face is a face you love

heaven waits
the clouds are rambunctious now
the light is estranged
the light is coy
the light presumes a galaxy

beginning 210 million year ago, mammals came into their own
scurrying and prowling with a mind of light under the light of the
moon..
the true oldest mammals are thought to have been small creatures
awake and active during the night...mammals do not become sluggish
but active in chilly surroundings...muscle movement generates
heat...continuous activity in the cold has always been a mammalian
trait...

sharp dilated eyes...

        care for the young...

                the heat within....

GAUTAM VERMA

In Rectified Night

I give you my word

this wait is your tryst,   your trust

at the trysting place
the sign that does not pass

between us

if I keeps the word I give

stutterance

writing . . . movement
into itself (& into itself . . .

it's in the difference
there's the relation

every poem entails a poetics

SUSPENDED
cancelled
held
deferred;
balanced
supported
evicted

of what it *unconsists* (of how it devolves)

how do wolves evolve
swollen selves slovenly loves
how solve the lowly hours
the slow surround

                    in rectified
night time of plenty
& lack

luck's
un
countable

                    the *verb* carries across

& of the indescribable can it still be said

by touching letters
in the closed book form
what impossible words

& would be resolved that would be
fixed & free

& then the space between us was insurmountable
the infinitesimal space between our fingertips

insurmountable

ERICA KAUFMAN

after "songs to joannes" by mina loy

i might shrug off this arm
rest and say, "do something active"
or drink this. strike rock. hold up
my hands. chlorophyll coated.
bitter. where only i expose.

I might disqualify vitamins
with colorful multiple choice theology
single out then redeem

* * *

i might let you take care
of something cosmic then later
rename it "presumptive signal"
then blame revelation and call
individualism unparalleled

i might accept the covers
later when feelilng less excluded
more chosen more plural

* * *

i might embrace all three
personalities the day you are born
and i own the system again
again i should drink this
because it's contemporary

i might turn interesting
one day after language burns
person and name is a verb

Holy Flight of Letters

It is the fiction of authenticity
Looted from the original and later carried
Out of antiquity

Enter: incarnate
How? We cannot inquire, it is meant
To baffle—blossoming or
Like a bolt

It is written:
A near time is coming
Of injunction

To read is not the dry land of supposition
I know a story of the desert, but only the beginning
A narrative laid out in brick

It is not certain
Which room or rooms represent a man
Carrying a lamb, dressed in
Splendor

But the door to the next
Room gives the visitor an idea of blue glaze
Independent of any brick

Beatrice will be your guide

You can hear her voice on the phone:
Go down these steps and you will find a train to Buckow
Is Buckow interesting?

It is interesting enough to exist
But does it have hungry men who look?
They are not being paid to look

If you are polite, they should treat you gently
They should welcome you openly as a man who comes out of
The world

It should be an open-ended ticket

The twenty-two letters of fire
The twenty-six letters of sleep
To conspire—with dregs of ink

The fig tree opens its flesh like a door
And the waters branch out from the Tree
And the calendar of days begins with flight . . .

Did the voice come out of the Tree?

The answer: this is why coffins are made of wood

In the cool of the day, His voice goes like fire

Objection: one of His days could last a thousand years

Thorns and thistles, but not delicious grasses

Rabbi asked: how could their eyes be opened?

The answer: this is the snake of plausibility

The proof: the Tree will not be seduced with proof

Our Rabbi asked: did God eat of the tree?

The other said: He gave the taste of death

Which translates: IT MUST NOT BE TOUCHED, for looking would not do

God tests with questions

And man is thrust out into the world

Being Holy!

Why did He not make her at the beginning?

He took the rib from its place inside of the man

The Rabbi asked: why was woman created by theft?

By closing up the ribs with flesh, he made of man a shroud

The Rabbi asked: so Eve was made of a bone?

The other asked: what has man lost by giving up a rib?

The rabbi said: he seeks the thing he has lost

One asked: why is she given such flowing blood?

The Rabbi said: if the man stands naked, the rib is hidden

Another asked: why do they walk in front of the corpse?

The Rabbi said: He built more chambers in her than man—

For He did not make her of the head, or the eye,

Or the mouth, or the heart, or the hand—He made her

Out of the rib: and out of each limb, He gave her

The order of Song

            The New Year
            Runs along the hem of a dress
            To the Sanctuary of a vanishing
            Euphrates

            Map of Babylon: a ribbon
            With a ring through the lips
            Of a prisoner

            The raw material
            Had first to be destroyed—
            Best evidence of an erotic hand
            The living waters of her leafy
            Zone

The living Foreskin speaks the truth, stamped on the Holy flesh of preference, the two great fishes of instinct: causing the rivers to flow: so twice he struck against the rock of blemish: it is written that by smoating the rock, we read of times to come: they looked at the stranger, who appeared to them like a hill, putting his head into the other's mouth: as a man sleeps, the soul creeps about, split as it is with dread: this is hinted in the ransom—of Epileptic night: the Pleiades, of her private parts: and so, the strong are driven out: this is the "tiny lights" we associate with trembling: like flies with nothing else: the animal-shape of likeness: just as the one who eats grass is an ox: the pillar of smoke: and, in consequence: THE DRY LAND APPEARS: bread can be a prayer, so can rock, but grass can never have the shape of man: we read in the Book of Fire: the name contains a woman, hidden from view, just as Cherabim lack a sexual beard: but does the ox gaze into the face of man? with branches of desire, thinking of grass, for such things show themselves to be true, and vanish: and

from this fired-forth the moonlike dark: radiance, a coupling of light
and dark: all on account of the moon (according to Cain) whom she
fucked like a flashing sword: He made her go down, as light into
marrow, still clinging to His side, she flew up and tried the gate: but
the Holy One cast her out—grumbling: this is the flashing sword of
origin: and her beauty led astray the Sons of Man: for it is the desire of
night to fasten itself to the light: the world is constructed on the
principle of an egg, whose fluid membrane gives

birth to desire: till the sun said to the moon, how can a little candle, no
more than an egg, having no light of its own, but only by charity—
vaporous: for the light of the moon is a throne not firmly fixed: and
this is the name we clothe in flesh: and yet the flesh would take the
shape of man, till the unclean man is robbed by light! it exhausts the
body: the broken book: the coats of skin: the poison-god of how many
letters:

In the dream:
The extravagance of a highway
Going out of sight.

If he is too long in the room
He seems to have the agitation of a dog:
It was nothing more than having forgotten to eat.
The visible is like a trapdoor in the sky:
One looks up and up

Making the eyes work for a living.
Today, we have the sun as companion.
Tomorrow too.

I promise to be strong as I go out among the bricks.
Hold nothing back, freshly shaved.

My errand is to operate like a wave far out at sea.
And yes, bricks do close, one against the other.
At other times, they don't.

Being mute.
I'll sit in the sun, taking things up:
Stirring with a spoon, looking at a napkin.
These are the choices I like.

At the door you are given a voice. Which voice? You can only have your own voice. This is our specialty. All that you see has been done by hand: the lights, the tables, chairs, the sun outside the door, the shadows full of sparrows! It's all completely real.

The man kept coming by:
It's a thing that happens—if a stranger
Finds her attractive.

But what he
Wanted was for her to tell him:
How could she know
What it was?

She was a woman.
This is the truth of discovery.
But what did he want?

He said he came for a name.
What she sold were empty books.
And he was a writer.

Could she tell him a story?
She put her arms behind her head.
The better to think.

On Sunday
At the end of the day
She took a walk.

This is what she told him:
He had no idea if she walked alone.
She only said that she walked.

Did he know the hill?
Yes—he knew the hill.

This is the hill of descending light.

The hill is not any hill,
But rubble-hill.

He did not know of any light.
He did not know of any song.

He had only seen the woman in a room of empty books.

Because the light of a hill does not sing—of work.
Woman work.

And a mouth crawls out of the Tree. To speak: would you like to see a
little house? It's far too small to vanish. Not knowing what it is to
want: man aspires to the condition of being like a boat. It's easy
enough to understand why a soldier would sit next to a milk can, but
how do we explain away the clarinet? Look into the mouth of Capital—the thing itself, or a sky upstairs. This is where a friend ought to
enter: like a visit in the night, setting out on voyage in the park. We
have come for a monument—constructed out of the logic of a grave,
or lights going out toward the Spree.

Who is speaking?
Who has the right to speak for others?
To weigh and measure?

And say the yes of no.
How much stone can you carry?
How many stones is the walk?

Would you like to meet men of leaves and naked branches?
The wondrous tribe for whom a stone is always only
A stone

Yes—finally
Like pigeons drawn to the sun
These are men with whom we will be happy
These are men who only make

Walls of utility
Did I say walls?
Tents?

Yes—walls
So easily taken apart by
The good, round stones
Of consequence

Very good + copy in gray linen, stamped in gold. According to the testimony of his companions, Kafka was correcting the proofs on the night he died: of blue ink, creased twice (horizontally and vertically) with folds slightly torn, but without damage to the letters: pencil on verso. The Holy Place—becomes itself by being rubble: as if by miracle, the lamp burnt for 8 days. Under the compulsory name of Sarah.

Let me tell you about the garden. At the bottom of the wall is a green of fired brick. After that, everything is white. She has made a garden out of things scrubbed by light. And the best part of a floor is sand. I wanted to question an inhabitant: to see if it changes with time, but no one was about. So how did I know the man who makes things in leather to be so far away? The answer: seven wires are reaching up the wall. These will—in a time that is yet to come: be lost in vines. This is the garden of being completely new. And the vines will also flower. But an Architect must be pragmatic: to make a place that works. It should not wait: impossibly. She has built a place of the most auspicious brick. It too has a tree at the center:

Amelencia Canadensis

Will the woman who was here yesterday come back?

I'd like to lean against her delicious walls:
By keeping to the shade of a tree, I move about in the length of a day.
When was the street named?

Does its name reflect the passing time?
Next to the broom, I would have clean windows
And speak of cold water.

This too will be part of another day.
I will try and locate—by touch.

According to tradition: both males and females, Jews and non-Jews, work under a light of frugal decoration: a rabbinical halt in the day. Objects rescued from the rubble show us how to read. This is what the strong man does—being faithful. But for many years the river was forbidden. Why forbidden? One must look the other way. The Rabbi said: if you enter into the dark, can you say—which is the Tree to open?

She said: I will give you a map. And in the margin is also written, a heaven of folded letters: out the window of her room, a tree. But go back three years: in a very public action, at the end of tranquility, each man or woman, will be granted: a machine that writes! One has only to schlep it up the stairs. For the strange man must give of a woman: the machine that writes. But follow: on either side is salt and pepper. Next position: an apple, native to the Tree of Berlin. Approximately nine or ten months old. And drying from within, the apple of the apple: for surely, if we are to be saved, and not Utopic—few know what it means, the place cannot be reached. But the apple is happy, being an apple, nesting among the letters. In the final position: approaching coitus, her bed is adjusted to sleep. At the top of the machine is a chocolate insect: a May beetle wrapped in foil. Looking straight out—

This is
What I like about your body,
Being next to mine
Or apart.

It is in the flesh,
We find ourselves most
Vulnerable—It is in the flesh
I pull you apart.

I like how your teeth work.
How your face is marked by the light.
I want to talk into you.

I want to be inside.
This is the reason I want you to be.
It is not a question of delight.

But of going away.

Being private.
How does a body escape from the State?
It may not be found out.

We have signed ourselves into flesh.
And it is your body—I want.

To take you with delight.
And know you, again and again.
In all your places.

EDWARD SMALLFIELD

(the classics)

<pre>
                              Ichor
        & human   emotion:
          an ocean
       of glitterings   an arbor
    (pleached?)   (bleached?) between the harbor
         the twin   potions
    of language   of skin   a mention
       of mending   the sore
          hours   the days
                         of August
                          of dust
                  now I   pay
         a history   blurs
         the summer   surrenders
</pre>

(after WCW)

        I have eaten
the reddish
        purplish,
            beat
hell out of   the earth   under our feet
                        , sluggish
                                    contagious
the stiff   curl of wildcarrot   leaf
                            cannot express
                                        rescued
under the surge   the blue
                                    some hard-pressed
    house   of September
    isolate   after deer

(carrer de París)

balcony = eyelash

some anonymous architect
wrought-iron wreckage
unfashionable
as nakedness   nobody mentions
a page
almost transparent   a wedge
this hour   between   the past tense
& the present   to teach
an English
: a wish
to reach
for   what trembles
within   *atardecer*   what crumbles

(Gràcia)

```
                                              The text
of these streets:                                  graf-
fiti       in red        & black       , the laugh-
ter      & voices            &              wreck-
age                 &                         sex:
the slender                                   half-
hour              between              the graph
of sun            through              the next
sky:                                           life
                                       is a membrane
porous                                  & stained
with yesterdays:                             eyes
                                            linger,
something      is given off             , clings
```

Waltz

(you   listening   (to

inside   a dress
     played as

                  cello
a waltz is

                      & fours
the drummer   sweeps the floor
a white

              in August
stained with
peaches

                 sweat
    teaching
        something
                the act
under

             a red
      definition

             isn't

KRISTEN HANLON

The Specified Mapping Is an Invalid Path

*

Without a kiss,
without any kind of warning,
he melts back into

the maddening crowd.
The mock funeral procession
passes, followed by

dancing reapers
(shouldn't the reapers
precede the coffin?

oh nevermind).

*

Was blind to alternate routes,
ignorant of other paths.

The young couple embracing
in alley-light
should make me wistful

or nostalgic, but
I'm only tired.

*

Later, after most
have gone home
or to the movies,

the effigy-burning.

*

"Through" is not "across"
but it tries hard
in the dream.

King Friday: "Surprises are not
for understanding!"

*

At the reading, a poet insists
on referring to his poems as "texts":

"In this text I was trying to…"
"I wrote this text in Denver…"

For this, I paid
a babysitter?

*

Without a kiss,
without any gesture
of pity, I proceed

to crash through
the undergrowth.
Vague ferns everywhere.

"It's dinosaur time!"
the cheery guide announces.

*

At the bus stop,
dirty-raincoat man
whispers:

"When otherness estranges,
take heart!"

*

The only mommy
in a sandbox full of
nannies.

My feet itch, but
I can't take off my shoes
for fear of sending
"the wrong message."

*

There's a boy twirling
an imaginary lariat;
a girl grimacing

for apparently no reason.
And my boy playing
quietly, for a change—

*

*But what am I
to do, what
am I to you?*

STEPHEN VINCENT:

from **Sleeping with Sappho**

4

                         ]heartless
                         ]tentative
                         ]I will not
              ]not for you
              ]darkness
                         ]
                         ]the footfall
                         ]
                         ]pure crimson
                         ]

6

not
]

]
]
]
]

stop   [
invisible   [
         ]
          does not

her bare throat   [
]
no gold
]
no

12

]
]
]
]thoughtless
]her sandals
]
]double-knotted
]
]

16

Some women dream rabbit, three in shadow,
Three in light
And there are others who only a wolf inside the door
Few dream what hates

Hard to confuse many by one
For the woman, call her Carrie,
Who stays constant, leaves no one

Behind the door, silken among roses
Yes to her lover and yes again
  No to abandonment, no
  To the rabbit's fondling fur

                In a dark
                lightly

                The silhouette
                She who arrives.

16 Alt.

One woman says a soldier with a goat
    Another says a soldier with a fox
And I say it is rarely the one you are with
    But how you hold new love in your arms

It is difficult not to be confused
I have been defeated by many
Less beautiful (Sylvia)
Who found me not

Nor would she sail to Crete
For me nor our other lovers
Nor did she offer clear wine or Iris—

        Out on her own

        The dark
        Her shadow faint

        I must forget everyone:

Why she would not rather see my wanting face
    The cut light across the peach in my hand:
Rather the fat soldier exiled from Ithaca
    Routed and scarred purple by Odysseus

] may that she not return
]
] part my arms
]
] outward
]
] expectant

Rope the Oak tree
Brave one

Gather bitter lemons
And then some

And for you
Lay away

Shut up
Speak to no one

I will arrive
Rude, crude

You will be the last,
Burnished.

63a

Lie down
On an alabaster pillow

Little devil, take my
Pleasure blended as a pearl

I will give you
Into a bed of small gods

Tiny features in their faces

Dimples and seizure.

ELISE FICARRA

From **Counterspell**

light comes out of the word but does
not remain. angel files his nails
adjacent rifle. corpses speak. "the
names are tense." "they asked to be
given form and were scattered." you
can't see the horizontal line running
across the sky but it's there. the
question comes from an infinitely far
space. the part of the circle you
don't see because it's where you're
standing. "his house of light." "we
would have loved each other too
much."

rock the color of blood. gills becoming ears. elocution. suffusion. "our hut." "you can go in if you want." slackened rope. shed becomes boat. construct river, oars. form making limit visible. "not one without the other." the enemy was a hoard clearing the hill. "we rowed o how we rowed." "saw them as they were seeing us." slitting hash marks on her wrists. "stroke." "coveted spot." madness let loose. water beading under her skirt.

"everyone misses the light." "you said yourself it was unrecognizable." "I lend you my ear for mishearing." "so we part in order to meet." "the debt of another." philosophical avoidance. the bartender's gaze. "are you willing?" "to look back." bodies careened from the vehicles. hit the ceiling. floorboards. we set up a camera to show the means of its making. "henceforth becomes insolvent."

"stand alone. eat the poison flowers." "I am unsure." "I want to betray him." "the body's two sides." "mists." "you are above rather than under my standing." "devil's vex." "cobblestones from heaven to heaven." "light packed up her caravan." "unbinding." "the space we cross." "a proposition." "unfold this fabric." "a carpet." "nearly continuous warfare." "blossoms."

dark wood for baths and wandering.
cocaine destined among which oil and
diamonds. the object in its absence.
intercepted migration patterns.
forgetting are certainly. this memory
is thus. darker and their shadows
applying rulers and razors. law's
nature to infringe. n's mystic pool.
money seeps out. transnational smells
and ferment. the shit pile. flies
devoted to a private life. "you owe
me." "these are my standards."

"you do not fall in love with a puppet" mother sd. "because you know some evil puppeteer is pulling the strings.". "but she could not *not* fall in love with the puppeteer" G-d was behind this and behind that smiling falsely of false god. "desperation to exchange" "houses for horses." "something remains." "tokens." "skeletons." "float the bones." "pasture." "Fire." "everything they say about me is wrong." (proof)

"in making me in your image you
destroyed yourself." (proof) "I
became city." (proof). "not only."
(proof) "I wanted to write you from
the center of a nerve." "I wrote you."
(proof) the dead begin to
wander. achieving conversion.
"providing conditions" "of
impossibility." "dis-enchantment."
"blood was running among the names
I gave to your name." "it went crazy."
"it was a splendid weapon."

"choose a remedy." "give me that vial." "poison belongs to no one." "it is a gift changing hands." "our commonality." "this isn't an argument." pressurize contradictions. heat withdraws from the object. "such as colors, tents cloaks." "that meteor." "he carried his head." "thus meaning escaped" "draught of arsenic" "a reign of fascination" "imposed in the manner of a wound." "beloved."

managing the image we forgot what it's for. "what do you think?" "sorcerer's apprentice." "exactly." "illness or the back of the wall." "dark spots in the lungs." calculates inner dimensions of an urn. thoughts hawked on arrival. funeral. G-d accused of shirking. her face a lash. "strong-buy recommendation." bugs filled our throats and noses. assumptions about the nature of humans. "among which property."

G-d speaks "its been lonely" an equation with two unknowns. tracking shot. ssush the baby to sleep. "you have seen nothing." "forgetful creature." like family. simultaneously neglected and suffocated. "so you can be smashed and keep going." "answering." "answered." sKin. and this. pricK. "weighted and light." "lighted and weighed." Kiss'd. thickest. playing poKer. "how I loV'd all that you sd."

ANTHONY HAWLEY

Oughtabiography

returning to chairs
not quite right
at what rate
disappearance
sets in
swirl
perpetuates
a sense
gets closer
to what
there's really
only furtherance
now how to weasel
out of vanishing

triangulated tertiary
restless appearance
one who was
to have been skilled
in some sport
proceeds directly
to the gala
of pronominal
disguise
camouflage city
city of wishing
light was shed on
a whole thing
to ambulate
the end

a head
halved
promised to drift
latitude approximate
incision ensures
severed relations
with remembrance
as the ordinary
continues to walk
the rims of vats
one is left with
pursuit of splitting
identifiable faces
mouth the forking

itinerary
at what point
one does
not return
to an understanding
of oneself
voluminous
arrangement
myth-infused
to the touch
conglomerate
of caught wandering
all my museums
would probably agree

little is new
with a face
appears only
to be partitioned
some singular
aspect split
heap of what
cannot
be exercised
past a portion
is all
after all
is washed of
speculation

with spectral
outnumbering
there are only
gaps any given
moment trying
to materialize
from living cities
of violent address
the lapse between
breath doubled
loops around
the frame or what
a body ago
was still

story
undone
somewhat speech
emptied argonaut
stenciled supplement
is what is
after shutter
exposure
quotation
tattooed
to seared
skin eyes
in the failure
to articulate

night
poleaxed
body's dim
geometry
of clanging
rumor
grid
one was
and not
architecture
asking
asthenia
to quell
the atlas

of choice
is there any
the doubling
leaves less
sense what
was to have
been complete
insoluble
growing
into nothing
but things
rule are
young
usurp one

another's place
given over
spectacular increase
eventual facet
every room
of the head
comes to
purloined
chrome context
restores
all the soft
science of glued
sayings

rebuilt circumference
imitating
ghost city transparent
intimation city
succession
of parts
in abundance
sum
of solitudes
head's paradox
some
dumb luck
to have been split
to build bereft

fortress
infinite
accretion
of unchanging
interval
binding
head
in stitched
chronicle
fully formed
blocks
not gone
but fashioned
from one's resemblance

DAVID ABEL

Lebanon

*The motif is always the same: a female figure with a significant book.
Bodies are the truest sense of words. The intention of the glossary is
not simply to provide a guide to words and forms that do not occur;
literary coexistence has proved a doubtful asset in the history of poetry.
The decay movement has been unable to advance beyond Scotland in
Monopoly. At least in part coterminous with their own vividness, the
speakers like Latin, English, Arabic. Though its scent suffered a number that threw out backs, the various strongly marked disruptions followed themselves in reverse, left to themselves, radio.*

Introduction

Open any book. Your good nature will bring you unbounded happi-
ness. It would probably not be possible for human beings to perform
this—Accept the next proposition that you hear. To go back to the
mountaintop. Oh cold wind my hands forget everything. On the soft
and dirty rooves of the city, I forgot. I searched for what was lost, in
the lonely rooms of handsome strangers, in the dreams of embarrassed
immigrants, in the architect's sky with its well-designed clouds—which
have lost something as well. I am haunted—by numbers that repeat,
pursued by mechanical darkness. Someone will come to tell this story:

> *A vine cluster. A lock of light. Hold on to the locks of its hair.
> She curls the locks of my hair with her fingers. When it comes
> to grow green. The leaves were very green. A green dream. We
> have planted the greens by the water of your spring. The green
> shade. A green note. The green nights. Your green eyes. The fire
> erases and eats away its greenness. The most costly vegetables.*

Open any book, close the first and open another. You become the story. The book is only something lost, a boy who died a child, the night crowded with vacancy. Implacable stories. No number disappears, the lights go out but the number three repeated three times, the number one repeated four times, the number twelve repeated twice—I turn the lights on and off by thinking about the numbers. Someone is sending me a message: *Care draws its lines with an iron nail.* Of what use to me are eyes that do not see you?

1.

O old nest,
my toe-nails
break and here
are the monuments of kings

St. George tends her blind father's grave
stretched out at your feet
like a cobbler hiring a hut
(24 instances noted)

O rose, take care—
take my ribs as a couch—
for her brother who is dying
we sold my sister's amulet

O organ of the nights,
four white rabbits
whose heads are like those of cauliflowers
shall strip (the leaves of) the myrtle

O for her sweet land and for those hills,
the foundation stone,

the captive bird,
the smell of a dead lion

I have no companion but you;
at the mention of your name
a thousand peacocks march in Asia

the rust is eating
a carafe full of red wine

she has been doing this for one or two years

and if you blow up the fire
it thinks that you belong to it

O mother of men,
I want to dance—

what is the matter?

In his hand is a book;
it may be the New Testament.

A thousand and one sighs for a draught from a jug.

Meticulously cutting his nails
he warms his eyes on our cheeks
prematurely

asking,
What use is the world?

2.

Barud,
faithful dog,
guardian of the orchard,
our lamp is failing

Hoarseness of autumn in its chest,
a parrot babbles on top of its cupboard,
a slipper gleams on its foot
like the seas of your eyes.

3.

Who scraped in the snow with her hands
saw fortunes; digs in the ashes,
a sky filled with perfumes

Decay has set in on
that dark blue and splendid iris;
I should not exchange this mill of ours
for the world.

4.

Wild mint
outside the house

no one knows what he wants to say
(35 instances noted)

5.

Never again shall we listen to the green curtains,
the orange peel old and blotchy

In my land is the porphyry—
I search this world for you.

The land of the lightning—
the world searches itself for you.

A veil of locusts—
the world goes round and round.

A pool of wine—
it is all pools of tar.

At the end of that garden
he spits red blood
on the rugs.

Wrapped in black headdresses
the white butterflies fly
in a temple that has collapsed on itself.

Like crystal in the moonlight
the carcass of a mule
full of acorns stained by red wine,

parsley and lettuce,
early red roses making the stones of the houses weep.

No bee remains in the hive.
A crow is swallowing the corpse.
Coming from the land of Persia:

no sweet girl, no songs, and no wine.
To build castles in order to warm you,
a thrush is building a nest in the woodwork of a coffin.

6.

On the day that we were created
the swords turned pale.

The scents of our clothing exhalations
of pistacchios and hazelnuts.

Your brown body
a worn and faded rug
dazzling with its diamonds

It may be that it occurs to the world to moan.

A rose seller sold this Paradise at a loss.
Falsehood had laid its eggs—
between you and me.

7.

A parrot babbles
her hoop still clatters in the mist

wood of coffins
from the gold dust of your body

thus you leave the world.

Here is an abandoned bell.
Why this weariness, this trout?

It snows wine.
July is drowning.

New York City, 1990

*This homage/travesty, which forms the third section of an ongoing series,
Orbis Pictus, draws materially on* The Poetic Vocabulary of Michel Trad: A
Study in Lebanese Colloquial Poetry *by M. C. Lyons and E.I.Maalouf
(Beirut: Librairie du Liban,1968).*

*Michel Trad (1912-1998), whose poems were widely memorized, and some-
times served as lyrics for songs by Fairuz and others,published many books
of poems, often reprinted; he worked for more than thirty years as an
administrator in the Roman ruins of Baalbeck in the Bekaa valley.*

COLLEEN LOOKINGBILL

The Committee

*"When the only tool you have is a hammer,
everything begins to look like a nail."*

　　　Lotfi Sadek

how ovalike it is—if shape selects perception
neural networks transmit traditional dogma
some variety of origins have collapsed
thrown the dice as in learning from life

experts never in short supply, we appointed
four types of non-specificity
　　1) confusion
　　2) newsstands
　　3) political crime
　　4) basic ambiguity

this explains how we see color
white cool and black warm
we can't just say blue—say "lt. blue" or "med. blue"

given such free and easy treatment of words
the committee begs Socrates to clarify justice

too many bad decisions ensue, try toning it down
in fact you don't need to talk much
just listen—elemental ticking of a cell

our heartbeats slow down, speed up
controversial cars leave intersection like creosote bush
ordinarily you might have to adjust
icy road at night slashes learning time considerably

in degrees of truth there's exaggeration
from a slightly improvised human operator
seeking another place where intuition ignites

verbal rules installed in sullen tunnels
evidence of perspiration, panting
stairway doors open—elevators hard to come by
smooth ride through solace of uncertainty
mind blending with invisible frequencies

draw inverse personal opinions, skirmishes by hand
it's just a fad—provisioning nothing for something

Interregnum

The living present, space and stars a convincing place to live. All things change uncanny self-acceptance of intimate relation, boundless frame our being, our freedom. Sometimes circumstances, sometimes woman—our bones and nerves arise in a position of time. But it is night, I am lifting countenance deep in the far country, exposure sends me re-inventing nocturnal worlds, so much has been collected, remains exuberant, the whole row at once a politics of refusal.

Second visit muffles supple effect of movement, spontaneity of dress, quick response inventive direction, thoughts fly off and then rebound to vanish within buoyant discretion itself. I hold open a door, subtle expedition magnetic pull. Walking homeward, caves of sleep, the topography fused with wind's flurries, wings closed, skin a shade paler covered with diminutive mesh strands the color of smoke. Now I know sheer expectation dense and warm against tendrils dim with pollen.

Getting out is not so difficult, each new surface becomes more and more uncomprehending. Bring back talk—against Nile green candles into empty books, illustrations in my blood about alchemy and stones. Why shouldn't all of this be there, it must be somewhere, perfectly visible and numerous as a thousand clandestine recipes thinking if we believe completely, something always occurs.

No pain, no separation, no betrayals in my native city, no clocks, no calendars to wash away the long journey. No details, no explanations. Time by the throat, speech a hot wave, sing or shout words into the future where fear shrivels to ash, face filled with eyes drowns concealment. Narrow stretch of terra firma, scarcely ripple of little creek remarks on heron and her flight. I'm at a loss what to do thinking the world I describe does not exist, image so carefully in mind all the trans-Siberian voyages out my finger tips.

Shielding agile seasons my hand pulls the cord, opal shade morning light, pages of complications, this terrible doubt, some unexpected proof. Our album of devotions—murmur of constellations with you in mind. Sense of ample graciousness circling the crowd, I walk between the benches in the little spaces, stand upright among memory's intoxicated emotional radius like the compass of this story. Link between morning and evening star ritualistic past with no writing paper to match pearl gray rain. Who has been here before to tell us we see a tremor of life in everything.

Elements gain sense, my moisture rises with the breeze, turning the wheel, arriving with different dawn. Sun in me I have lost my country, my name, one ecstatic shredding and slicing the mound of time, silver dress floating in it's element, torn fabric mended with threads of language. I have become someone else in the eyes of the world difficult to remember—features about to vanish, baffling counter currents of pain, until the book suddenly to pieces. Yes— I was grown up walls of prejudice, pressure of active hostility, tendency to slide back realms of civilization après le deluge. All these years nothing is ever finished, swept away by intensely luminous vision.

Invitation to dream while the cloud is on us, a blossom without reality or meaning. Try to reconstruct my face a framework of drum beats, tears and clinging. My body swimming and flying, sound of rainfall middle eye—new world, unfurled, arranged, dissolved, becoming open for the first time. No one is surprised smell of sandalwood and tobacco through labyrinth of confidences, a silent intermission absorbs convergent liveliness.

When it is all over dividing line new citadel breathing respite, period of recovery. I am loyal, alert, do not wish the world to perish, we watch and listen throbbing self-conscious, exact mood fused tender and mocking. Promise of return quite vanished, occasionally reflects back unsleeping reconciliation. From this beginning spread out, gain impetus from undeniable refuge. Suddenly stream going up then going down, our birthright re-papered, sustaining hope to out-dazzle final comfort quite clearly jabbed into consciousness. Passable thunder has time to stay, sparse territory proving innermost concern. This scene has chosen a second heartbeat, embodies heavy earthlike sand, gained picturesque half-obliterated, stranded here in the sifted evening.

Death Is the Mother of Beauty

so steady my circling

cicada crow cricket

dark soon become dance

lift speak sonorous shell

bending gentle

becomes you fasten skin to more

make it grow rings around itself

glow

in the middle of the

mad dashing

metrical dodge and weave

hot-wired a jingle

tap into this sap

she keeps the beat

kept her promise we

daily all devoured

generally more than we bargained

four brass knuckles white sheet

as in tuck me into

a delicate corner

dirty lace bones

in pale shade collectable

lip filth pink flesh

pry into

perfection twofold

eyeing

embedded brass tacks

hack into her secret

steel drawer

sew the story

uglier even than bodies

broken spilling

sipping something

sitting pretty

bench breathe better than ever before

boys trading birthdays

for body bags

ammo agriculture

avalanche pale mounds

purpler to go slipping into

halo harvesting

murmur me

memorize this grip

gag me, gorgeous

goes the adage

always

so sweet

goes the adder under my sleeve

believe me when I beg for it

lungs filled water foul pellet breast meat bitten into

the hue of blood the way it puddles

under her eyes

swivel

trough to middle

America

mid October blunt boards

creak

under feet a sawed-off stoop

rocking horse sloppy rocking be nimble crack skull

risk brittle entire while

so when she says

gasp

this word

does not mean what
you think it means

whimper

so bask in this

JOSEPH LEASE

from **Day By Day**

American Dawn

"Stay the course, we must not give up"—(drunken frat boy leaves country in ditch)—someone is taking a country, someone is taking his country, her country, our country, and trashing it—I mean, nothing's ever that stark, but this is stark, pretty fucking stark—the war: trying to "fix" their country at gunpoint—"this is our country": "this land is your land, this land is my land"—bunk wrapped
in

      hooey, hooey wrapped in
bunk—

—he keeps a note on the refrigerator, he wants to keep
going, memories crack like fantasies, scraps of story,
scraps of picture. Mouthfuls of wet, sweet cups of desire,
he gets the pictures, tries to guess what he's worth. If at
first you don't succeed, try, try, try again. Remember that?
God, what a sweet sap he must have been.

                            You know . . .

it gave him comfort.

        We're going back home to
Faith pushes through the money

We're going back home to every vote counts we're changing
The rules we're expecting disaster funding the nightmare sure
Starve the poor try our new prayer try our new blue Sunday
Try our football game and turn off the shooting try our
Daydream

Try our new rights
You have the right to
                              Remain silent

We were going somewhere, and it was falling down, and everywhere stars fell, and much better satisfied now, blue, for a while, for a while—elm trees and summer and birch trees and sky, elm trees and summer and birch trees and sky: how did I get here and where do I go, won't you forgive, won't you just see me, won't me forgive me, won't you just try—*"the TV is that of the US, the music is that of the US"*—I like that you can go into the drug store and buy canned soup and potatoes au gratin and Bumblebee salmon and pecan whirls and Jefferson was horrible and everything rolls by, a great river rolling, courteous, overwhelming, what is going on inside his head: "Indeed I tremble for my country when I reflect that God is just" (Thomas Jefferson)—

Expensive houses, expensive houses dying: I recognize the
voices—let's begin America or something, let's invite
everyone—America, you can't be greed, America, you're only greed,
America, one extra summer night—he wants to (you know)—feel like
a giant eyeball—

Oh I

Need you're so soft

Lavender
      Sky

Sky
      Like whiskey

Close your eyes: you're in a kitchen in a trailer, an apartment complex, a tiny house near the river, close your eyes: there's a dog in the yard—somebody got lost—a long time ago—somebody who was going to be here: dead man lying by the side of the road, could you almost see, could you almost see the moon—and the crowd in Kansas—and the sunlight was in their bodies—it was sound, it was voices, dividing, joining, trying something, making all the usual wonderful mistakes (hey I need you, who are you)—human forest in my city, dream money, we give each other life, human city like a vacation made of fire, we all guess night wrong—your eyes like rain—we all keep living—God I'd love to love inside your eyes—words like rain, eyes like rain, smile like rain—

Leaves on grass, astonishing sky, true as water—might as well, might as well let night in—if the story is falling apart: high school football, Miss USA gone wild, "the war on Christmas," we live in the house then we can't anymore— the town in summer and summer and sky and if I was desperate and if I just tried and if I was desperate I wasn't sad yet—

Cold wind blows in
Cold moves the curtain
      Hey breathe like snow
In the air just

Traces of snow in the rain hey breathe
Like

Rain in the wind

forty—six to fifty—six, fifty—six
to sixty—six, sixty—six to seventy—six, seventy—six to
eighty—six:

Well, you breathe a kind of dream: how will you, how will she, how will he—live—get through—bear up—whatever you want to say: dreaming of pictures of welcome and living, dreaming of pictures of shoulders and hair—America, you can't be greed, America, you're only greed, America, one extra summer night—

Want my

back porch, want my front porch, want my milkweed, my willow tree,
want a new body, want a new mouth, Christmas tipsy, kiss, yes—

I want to live forever, why not, why

not admit it—

DEVON WOOTTEN

from **"Landfall"**

Rather

The hymn

The hummed edge

Your hands part

Thirst

A bit of glass at your feet
tends to me

As one shrift
sends for his son

A question
Ethed & Lamed

Your moist lip

As I spoke
Thy moistened lip

My inked over-eye
whispers the chorded sphere

Your ax splits
the breath—room

My feet stitched
slicked as through a cylinder

Plait unto skin

Your un-
wound

Re-and-re-
mounded

Your welted mouth
stumbles me

Lest I wander

Willows

Brittle-close

As the crops are gathered

Thresh my hands

Please as in

The wholeness of fruit as in

O depth
Stay with me

                                            Silt-blooms

                                            Many-hued
                                            as your lips

                                            Dried

                                            Crack

                                            A piece of bone

The river I knew

Constructed weather

Currents

A branch angled to shore

List the question:

Twine-betrayer
His the sod

Marvel the surface

Now
the divide

Furrows
between us

Birds
in the tall grass

Lift from me

Re-
spite

The garden
gone to seed

                                       Till in me
                                         your rough eye

                                         Fire in early spring

I am Considering Fire

There are wells to be dug

Father
This belled space

The orchard

This tree
cleft by lightning

As I would the earth

Abide

Linger me unto

Your hands

Quiet me

Though I have the one
I would not look too long

Feldsong

Noted:

sand
lungs
branches
bridges

Sunder

Allow artifice

Boats

Await my tongue

Of late
the Nowhere
-lowing Ear

Re-
sounds

Looms you
penitent

Ash-song unto each

You finger
the anchor-less word

Renounced

even air

dissolves

Hastens thy breath

As thou tendeth thy field

I carry measure

Fathom what weight

My hands passed

Bone-knit

Opacity flaked the sky

                Call the light
                    Plowed
                    under

                Guide
                the sower

BETTINA ROTENBERG

Dark Love

homage to Nathaniel Dorsky's Threnody

Dim lights   Half moon

blue-grey

white

I.

rising
band of
white

birth moves into death
grey light becomes fog

sun spot in flora
under water
lit up

looming blond brow
blue eyes recede
disappear behind scratched glass

                                                    each time
                                        the face I never saw
                                        before   this time

dark patches outline
sliver of
spider web with bean

pink/purple   red pencil flashes
lit

hand of stain
against thigh
foliage criss-
crossed

                                        fingers with angles
                                        lead to a Moroccan ring
                                        a sweet sweat lingers
                                        varnished empty surface
                                        that loves the crooked hand

sun on desert land-
    scape
sky with telephone
    pole

sun descends
darkness all around

There was fresh bread and cut oranges.

sun sinks into darkness
disappears in a
  small yellow band

                                We were lying on the floor
                                with our legs entwined.
                                His wife didn't seem to mind
                                our amorous gestures.

dead branches over
  light branches

branches — fall

                        I recall someone else in the house of semi-
                        furnished red rooms. A tall skinny girl.

slow pace
        interlaced thick branches

                                        Lips shut
                                  protecting eye
                                wide open, clear
                                      with other
                            churning eye in trouble

                            this beauty of conflicted face

start to move

man writes in one of two notebooks
  golden ropes against dark'ning sign

                              He was going to kill her one night.

        sikh
        God

                              He was lying on a couch
                        crouched down between two people.

lines of rope move

                              A woman came up to me,
                        and started to redesign the dress.

branches stir
beneath the ice
  arms against a light tapestry
    back-lit calligraphy

Asian child
& Asian workmen
winter on paper
bends towards child others walk
ghosts bound

                        She adjusted her orange shawl & said
                              I needed an orange dress.

Lit
red
bead-
like
carpet

clock shows 10:30
dark hands lit
by clock's low face

> I started to get on some
> bent skis
> & was sliding downstream
> when I saw what looked like
> turbulence & rapids. I thought,
> "O shit, I'd better turn around"
> but it was very hard to ski upstream.
>
> You were at the stream &
> (I think) you pulled me out.

dark) light) carpet or tree?

> *"I can't believe he gets a lot out of being irresponsible."*

red shapes light up &

fade with gems
into darkness
disappear again
in triangles, circles, squares

rays sweep
  across colors

disappear

                              I groped my way down
                              a winding staircase
                              to the first floor.

trees above trace
red & yellow
background

                              A drawing of a vessel
                              & writing pouring out.

trees   still
   upon
   light

                         He came into a hotel with his
                         arm around a tall blond woman
                                with a pointed nose.

                         When I said to them, "My husband
                         is sleeping with another woman," they said,
                      "No, she's hard and ugly, and has a pointed nose."

leaves slightly moving
sailboat in water
rainbow branches
overlay colors

autumn leaves on pavement

child's hand on glass

red stripes beside light
brown wood diagonally placed

> I never said a word at those dinners.

hand picks fish
in Chinatown

> The man was in a mental hospital
> because his father was a drunk &
> whored after other women.
>
> As a child he saw it all
> & rewitnessed it as an adult.

rocks, colors
blue over flesh

> I met a cult of women
> outcasts who made brightly
> colored dresses that were too large.

                    Like animals raising their front paws
                              they placed their hands
                        on the shoulders of a big man.

                              You invited me down
                              to a room with one wall
                              open to a lake.   I drove
                              my car, half-red, down
                              many terraced levels
                        to the edge of the water. Afraid
                              that my car might slip
                              into the lake, I folded
                              it up into a tiny toy.

patterns of netting
under water
branches move
burned & striped
black & yellow stars

move against handlebars
of bicycle

                        The building had many beds & no doors.
                        He led me to a small high bed in a room
                              with four or five people lolling about.

new spokes travel

                              I flirted with the men
                              & took my clothes off.

ponytail & white headband
on red

                    He saw my nakedness & removed his shirt,
                              laughing approvingly.

still brown-green flower
wrapping paper
light, red, bright, blue

                    He yelled at me, *"If you flirt with
                        everyone, stay away from me."*

flesh shapes
barely exist
dissolve into
black on white

patterns of netting
under water

                  (He loved me & I loved him & he flirted with me.)

                  He needed me to talk to—to have conversations.

black on white

leaves move slightly

      flesh, bark, tree in dark night

People like ghosts walking

cars & bus travel

"What kept trying to arrive in him was himself."

trees & fence
in front

statue of woman's face
and red lips

glowing green feather-fish

white cranes
structure of letters

S/
T/
R/
E/
T/
C/
H

interwoven branches
over water

I was in the Y & it was very late
at night & I couldn't get out
to go home. I was afraid he'd think
I was in trouble.
A slight young man

kept touching me. He seemed to want
to get me out by reaching the authorities.
But we couldn't speak to them.

Snow was piled high on all sides
and the night was lit by stars.

pussy willow & branch
against light—muted—
moving

She put her hand on his knee.

red wound
 pasted on trees

"*When muscles lock in spasm, go to the hospital
and ask for an injection of benadryl.*"

pattern on pavement

eye peering out
silhouetted windy branches
leaves in upper left

"I've considered your ideas and they have some merit,
but this is what I'm going to do. I've given it much
thought, and have to say I'm sorry."

stiff leaves barely
move in light & dark

visible
across the sky

"I suspect you'll have no trouble sleeping..."

red and brown lumpy surface
flashing into patterned   plane
  several new varieties
of red & black

rope with bell on
orange building

shadows light across leaves

nests
8-sided rainbow

blue dress
with other colors
emitting from it

They drift apart. They yell.
They come violently together.

light and green pocked
texture

light and shadow shiver
bubbles on surface

I was trying to draw a woman's face.
But she was like a mask.
I made repeated sketch marks
in three places. I saw a man with a key and saw
the woman again who had gone away
She had blue hair.
When I drew her face
it turned into a baby with eyes that looked up at me
with the sweetness of
a ripe persimmon.

prehistoric landscape
 preserved
  by snow

tree
fell

I dreamt I blacked out for two years, when I was 70.
I came to and everyone was annoyed. My mother was still alive. I
thought I'd lost my blue purse & my black purse.

Chinese child on court
catches ball & kicks it
laughs

Lights and blurred blue jewelry
in sky Sun is many-pointed
diamond   years
lighter and brighter.

                              Look away from the mirror
                              into the darkness
                              and see

Notes on the Poetics of the Serial Poem

Kate Colby

I come from a traditional greater-Boston family of the formal Sunday-dinner sort. They'll talk about anything but what they're talking about, then forget both. Textbook New England puritans, they are parsimonious to the extreme, which manifests in a practical anti-parsimony principle when it comes to the material, where time is infinite and resources are discrete. My parents will drive many miles to a cheaper grocery or hardware store than those in their town. When they go to Europe, my mother brings the dog to a relatively inexpensive kennel an hour and a half away. I joke that they'd drive thirty miles for cheaper gas.

Time confers no advantage; we are all in it.

Tom Orange

Serial form strikes me today as the form of choice for many poets working in alternative, avant-garde, experimental, innovative or non-mainstream traditions. Immanently versatile, serial form enables a shaping and ordering of materials into a product that can be open-ended or finite, sustained or discontinuous, procedural or intentional, or any combination or range therein. Inherently non-hierarchical, serial form rejects notions of the masterwork that underpin both the individual poem (as a discrete entity collected into a sequence or book) and the modern-day epic or long poem. Whereas these latter forms are marked by ambition, serial form is decidedly modest in scope and scale.

When traditional means of ordering aesthetic responses to human experience, such as mimetic representation in the visual arts or major-minor tonality in music, no longer prove fruitful, serial form historically has offered solutions that have proven generative; curiously though, the use of serial form in poetry seems to have remained fresh and abundant, perhaps in part by avoiding the limitations and dogmaticisms that surrounded it in other arts. Rehabilitating the serialism of Schoenberg and Webern after its war-era neglect, for example, Boulez and others fancied the idea of total serialism, which reigned so supreme for a time that subsequent composers (Stockhausen, Berio, Cardew, Ligeti, Penderecki, Reich) each in his own ways had to overcome it. Abstract expressionism perhaps achieved a parallel hegemony in painting, to which serial form merely posed one alternative or way out for Bochner, Flavin, Judd, Le Witt and others.

From the present moment, those artist's statements from the 1960s sound rather coldly rationalist and dehistorcized: Bochner's insistence on "solipsism," the "self-contained" and "non-referential" for example, or Smithson's "entropy," or LeWitt's "the idea becomes a machine that makes art." But I wonder if another of LeWitt's statements, that "conceptual artists are mystics rather than rationalists," isn't more often quoted than thoughtfully considered. Mark Daniel Cohen and John Covach have recently explored mysticism in LeWitt and Schoenberg, respectively. Flavin would have resisted such a reading of his own work, but I could not help think, upon viewing the "monuments for V. Tatlin" in the recent Flavin retrospective, that these were sigils from some future carrying a higher order of information. Or that all of Mondrian's work from 1920 onward might, when arranged properly, constitute a significant revelation. Serial form in poetry thereby joins music and painting in a field Janet Zweig has so thoughtfully delineated: ars combinatoria.

[References: Mel Bochner, "Serial Art, Systems, Solipsism," in *Minmal Art*, ed. Gregory Battock (New York: Dutton, 1968); Robert Smithson, "Entropy and the New Monuments," in *The Collected Writings*, ed. Jack Flam (Berkeley: University of California Press, 1996); Sol LeWitt, "Sentences on Conceptual Art" and "Paragraphs on Conceptual Art," in *Sol LeWitt: A Retrospective*, ed. Gary Garrels (New Haven: Yale UP, 2000); Mark Daniel Cohen, "Sol Le Witt's Rational Mysticism," *NY Arts Magazine*, May/June 2004; John Covach, "The Sources of Schoenberg's 'Aesthetic Theology,'" *19th-Century Music* 19.3 (Spring 1996); "Dan Flavin: A Retrospective," National Gallery of Art, Washington D.C., Oct. 3, 2004–Jan. 9, 2005; Janet Zweig, "Ars Combinatoria: Mystical Systems, Procedural Art and the Computer," *Art Journal*, Fall 1997.]

On the Sequence
Guatam Verma

Poetics, or the way words would disclose themselves about a need . . .
but, surely, a poem is its own explanation, its own reason for being . . .
Not wanting to tread where the poem does, a poetics that would not
be a poetics of the sequence, but a poetics of this sequence, every poem
entailing one, I proffer these, what might I call them, conundrums.

*

One writes from a certain lack, . . . with a little luck. Is one every free,
entirely, of narrative?

If each fragment the whole story?

[fragment: text from its context torn, a de-territory]

If time is the distance between one utterance and the next (never certain), then timing is what draws them into relation by dissolving that
distance, or by letting it dure, a certain duration. Theatricality.

How it all holds together, is that a too indelicate question? If there is a
theme, a thing to which the fragments cling, then it is themselves that
would announce it . . .

The sequence, for, yes, one reads sequentially, what would it delineate?
- not that linearity, but perhaps a being simultaneous, the map of a territory, deterritorialised

space the words would give us to see, and wanting it yet all to themselves, also perhaps, finally, conceal?

Not then of its constituent parts, and not of itself either, some other third thing the sequence would reveal, to make which appear, would it itself have to disappear?

The sequence: aggregate in a zero-sum game.

Its goal being interior to it (anterior), its beyond in back of it, what cannot reach, can only concede.

Peter Gurnis

Instead of thinking about the major American practitioners of the serial poem (like Blaser, Spicer, Duncan, Oppen, or Creeley), I invite you to consider two contemporary German poets: Elke Erb and Friederike Mayrocker, both of whom have been translated by Rosmarie Waldrop. Erb's early poems often have a feeling of the folk-tale hovering about them, and however elliptical they may be, always possess a kind of horizon line, which offers a temporary balance in an otherwise insecure world. In these poems it is as if Kasper Hauser were wandering about in East Berlin during the days of the GDR: "But there was nobody to do for him, he would have gone to the dogs: a field, an apple tree, a pond, a brook, an empty house." She is a poet who evokes a fallen world out of a few scraps. She does not employ folk-tale motifs to create a nostalgic view of the past. "Any living body that is cold and alone is unhappy," she writes. The poems do not appear to have been written as a series: each has a title, but the reader experiences them as if in a series. Her poems never work to create the fiction of an autonomous self who speaks, and in speaking, demarcates her own subjectivity.

    Elke Erb's later work, however, moves away from the simplicity of the folk-tale, the poems abandon any horizon line, and the reader plunges onto the vertical axis of language: that is, the ground disappears underneath our feet. The later work of Elke Erb increasingly seems to embrace the poetic practice of the better known Austrian poet Mayrocker, which is characterized by its rapid-fire syntactic disjunctions, ellipses, quotations, and montage; her work is multi-layered, obsessive, baroque, and yet it can also be light and transitory. Mayrocker's work is the definition of all that is gargantuan, opulent, and excessive. Her collage is not the collage practiced by the Modernists. Once at the Schiller National Archive, I watched a video of her at work in her studio, where she had all kinds of crazy strings running above her desk and what seemed like hundreds of slips of paper attached with paper-clips and clothes-pins: I could not but be impressed by the rich chaos of her method. At a certain moment in her prose text "Table of Matter" she writes, "TIME HAMMER : ARTAUD's poems which we read as if he, ARTAUD, revolved about us, a heavenly pillar of writing, as if he, ARTAUD, wrote his most grandiose heavenly thoughts here, above our heads, as if he, ARTAUD, performed such giddy heavenly acrobatics in the unfettered distance that it would take effort to keep up with his speed." Yes! To Mayrocker who summons the dead back to life. Yes! To Elke Erb, I wish she had a wider audience. In neither of these poets does one find the kind of serial poem as practiced in the U.S during the 1960s. Poets who find the idea of the serial poem useful might look to the examples of Elke Erb and Friederike Mayrocker. Parenthetically, it might be of interest to note that Mayrocker, is at the age of 82 often regarded as the Grand Old Woman of Austrian poetry, and her difficult, experimental texts hardly have a marginal status.

On "The Specified Mapping is an Invalid Path"
Kirstin Hanlon

Gertrude Stein in *Composition as Explanation* wrote "Beginning again and again is a natural thing even when there is a series." The serial poem is an ideal form for me now, as I am continually starting and stopping poems, coming back to them weeks or months later, trying to fit pieces together, rearranging and discarding. Only when I give myself over to the thought of abandoning something altogether do I find the wherewithal to try and rescue it. Sometimes it works, sometimes it does not; it involves a great deal of trial & error—not unlike motherhood

Stephen Vincent

Transversion is the word I apply to the process of making my particular kind of "translation." There are poetries—such as Ann Carson's *If Not, Winter (Fragments of Sappho)*—in which I find myself in some kind of automatic and antonymical dialog.

That is, I feel compelled to contest or offer up an opposite point of view. In the case of Sleeping With Sappho, where Ann Carson's translations point to the right, mine point to the left, black becomes white, etc. A better comparison to the sense of play—the act of writing—may be to a tennis match, or full court game of basketball. But, I should add, the ultimate intention here is not competitive in a destructive sense, but more like an active conversation, a dialog in which one work nourishes the possibilities and freshness of the other. If that is a stance, it is meant to be a good one, in which the history of literature becomes one vast fabric in which the various weaves constantly mirror—in this case, turn the fabric upside down—and redefine (light or dark) the possibilities of each.

Elise Ficarra

Counterspell started with a cube flattened on the page to a 4ʺ by 4ʺ square. The work required compression in order to happen. I was going through some things at the time, which means going through a body and I wanted to give that work another dimensionality, which became voices in dialog. The voices occupied and emanated from of a sort of bardo (cube). They were disembodied, doing the work the body does when the body is absent. Let me explain. I was reading Kathy Acker. I was visiting my mother. I was thinking about the forces that hold us in enchantment and wanting to pressurize that cube to find the cracks in the structure where things break-down and something happens inside the cube that exceeds the cube and breaks the spell, constituting a new body, which is among other things, the body of the audience receiving the work. Counterspell is meant to be delivered live, ideally in a small, dark setting so that the room in which the reading occurs reenacts the pressure of the cube and a poetics of going-off-the-page. The spell is extended via the distribution of a hand-made giveaway card on which a condensed version is encoded, giving everyone an artifact/object to take home. It is hoped that the poetics will thus continue to work in/upon new bodies and locales.

Note: the quoted material in this piece includes invented and overheard dialog as well as adaptations and appropriations of found texts with homage paid to Jacques Derrida's *Post card* and Michael Sells' *The Mystical Languages of Unsaying*.

All My Museums: On Serial Poetics
Anthony Hawley

Serial space is athletic space. Athletic because every poem, every object is always a constant point of reference. Each thing is a thing and another thing. Simultaneously inside and outside itself, every thing wants escape. I don't mean the speaker wants to escape herself, but the poem itself wants to escape the poem, its own form. The serial poem is not just the whole thing, but the whole deformed thing in constant flight. This is like a perpetual softness.

Serial space is attendant space. Attendant because every poem, every object is not just an on-looker, a spectator, but part of another poem, another object. Each thing is a primary and secondary thing. Simultaneously the foreground and the material structure, every thing wants in and out. I don't mean pieces of serial poems have a narrative relationship, rather each part wants always to get outside itself via the attendant, to pass on their function in vomit, shit, or transmutation. And not. This is like a perpetual becoming something else.

Serial space is hysterical space. Hysterical because the whole thing spasms.

Serial space is promiscuous space. Promiscuous because the attendant parts always withhold. Serial space is intermission space. Intermission because the poem is always in-between channels, shows, frequencies. Serial space is museum space. Museum because what is not fractioned, displayed? Serial space is residual space. Residual because the poem has no use except unto itself. Serial space is the mould of the body, the costume of all my distances. Serial space is the chilled organ, shelved, what edges I have left.

A Note About Lyric Sequences
Joseph Lease

Each lyric sequence creates its own music.

Each lyric sequence creates its own world(s).

"Free Again":

I could describe the sequence in order to emphasize disjunctive poetics, or I could describe it in order to emphasize continuity and return, repetition and variation.

When I read it aloud, it feels like a cascade of leaps, and it also feels steady and smooth.

The different sections of the sequence create/enact an emotional trajectory.

Here's joy: Why does one thing come before another, and why does still another come after that other one-

Like any piece of music, the sequence builds up emotional responses-

And narrative and critique-

Lyric structure becomes dramatic action.

A rite of passage made actual in a construct of words.

And that action, for me, becomes storytelling.

The motion from section to section can sing. One is very aware of (one is very in love with) the music. Different instrument voices take up the action in different places. Textures and layers and melodies and rhythms.

The music of the sequence enacts an emotional trajectory.

A form created to enact an "I" in places-rather than one place-the lyric self that stands in conflict. And the voices around us, through us, the culture. A sequence-as Cubist autobiography-can enact critique. A sequence embodies parts of a whole that is divided. A sequence can emphasize conflict. A sequence can embody struggle by division of itself. A sequence can embody struggle by forming, by coming together.

Conversation as story, music as action, not idealized synthesis.

Making.

Make it new.

Devon Wootten

Most poems I read do not doubt their own efficacy. That is to say, there seems little doubt that the poem will arrive at some sort of 'solution.' They move from A to B with few impediments. There is no moment of doubt; indeed, even their genesis seems unfraught. There is very little at stake in these poems. A poem must exist in crisis. Most poems manage only to write about crisis and end as quietly as they began.

This can be traced to three possible causes; 1) the poem is simply blissfully unaware of the tenuousness of its own existence, or 2) the crisis from which the poem speaks is so minor that very little linguistic energy need be expended, or 3) the poem is aware of the seriousness of the poetic endeavor and simply does not engage it with all the force of its being. Of these three, only the last is unforgivable.

The serial poem cannot take up the mantle of privileged speech. It denies its own wholeness because it would not stand against the void. The serial poem is consequential and therefore a gesture toward wholeness rather than an assertion thereof. The serial poem acknowledges the void and thereby engages it. It cries, "Something must be done!" all the while asking "What can be done?"

The serial poem is the egg in the duck that swims at the bottom of a well in a church on an island in the middle of a great lake. It would be found.

The serial poem would cease to speak. It would lapse back into the silence from which it came, but at the very point of wholeness, the place where it would give itself over to the other for consideration, it falters. It regards itself. All its efforts have been in vain—it has not brought sufficient linguistic resources to the speech-event. It must start again, "This as well" it says, "And this and this and this"

The serial poem is the not-yet-healed wound. At the slightest pressure, it begins to bleed anew. Much attention must be given to the wound lest it become infected. Water is boiled and bandages are cut from the bed sheets.

The serial poem is an utterance in crisis. It teeters between faith and despair. It labors. It fails but cannot resolve itself to failure. It reiterates. It stumbles. It staggers forward.

BRENT CUNNINGHAM

The Fourth Factory (Notes on Formalism)

What bothers a writer, what animates him or her into writing, is precisely the problem that writing poses—what writing is, what it might be for, its failures, its seeming impotence in the material world.

Delays and digressions are thus enmeshed in the written. In some senses writing is only the act of making time and circularity more apparent. As the writing goes forward, its delays and misdirections parallel the first desire of the mind: to go back and figure itself out.

It is not ironic that this has happened, that the idea (symbolized always by the writer) has grown alienated from immediatelife (symbolized by the receiver). In fact, this is exactly what speaking means: to break with the innocence of the pure listener, and thus with the immediate.

Viktor Shklovsky, the Russian critic and theorist, lived through an immediate of a rare kind. While surviving a world war, a revolution, and a civil war, he continued speaking. Time went forward for so long that Shklovsky accidentally became a memorist.

He and his circle were called Russian Formalists. The name can be misleading because they were critical of the terms "form" and "content." They preferred "device" and "materials."

These Formalists watched Stalin rise to power. It was not an era interested in delays or digressions. Instead the general intent was to speed things up, for the sake of production.

I would contend that, structurally, the memoirs Shklovsky wrote are actually digressions. Digressions in a major key. He assembled his works so that they did not blend, but appeared chopped up like frames in a film. As opposed to hybrid genres, Shklovsky wrote in stratified genres.

The American linguist George Lakoff talks about the way language can be used, either more or less effectively, to frame political issues. This can sound "formalist" because it takes language as an object. It imagines that some of the system of language can be affected or apprehended from a position outside it.

Shklovsky and the Formalists worked out taxonomies of literary works with the aim of explaining how they functioned. Their formalism was also an attempt to make a system of a system, and has something in common with Lakoff.

But Shklovsky stands opposite Lakoff as well. It's the delay or disorder, the break with system, that structures the formal manipulations. Which is the same as admitting: language is not an object at all, but a perception.

To choose a word is also to be chosen by a word. Or: to measure the effectiveness of language is like measuring the thought of ideas.

In one of his books, Shklovsky describes the stages of his life as factories. He says that time and political forces are "processing" him, as a stomach might process food.

His first factory was his early life, his family and schools. The second was the literary group OPOYAZ, his fellow theoreticians, his friends.

The Third Factory, it isn't hard to guess, was Stalinism itself. Eventually Shklovsky found a way to preserve himself, which was by compromise. He renounced his previous views often and then even more often. As a result it's quite hard to establish Shklovsky's "real" views on aesthetic theory. But maybe not any harder than establishing the view of any thinking creature.

For some reason love was not one of the factories that Shklovsky names. He did write about love however. It was in a book called *Zoo: Or Letters Not About Love.*

It was almost ten years ago that I stopped believing words could act as surgical instruments. It was a hard thing to face, and I began looking for a way to accept my disappointment. This didn't happen overnight. But eventually I did accept it. That is to say: I was eventually digested by it.

There are restrictions in language and thought which process a person as much as circumstances. This is a kind of fourth factory to add to the list. Where the first three factories make the person, the fourth factory unmakes the person.

This factory could be called the unthinkable. Inside it are the delays and digressions that also give language its order.

One thing I had to accept: in order to use language, it must be conceived as a single and whole thing, even though we can only find it piecemeal. For instance take the metaphor of the factory. It evokes assembly lines, workers with grimy faces, tools, machines. By these physical pictures the factory lends sense to abstractions: childhood, friends, political oppression, the unimaginable. But it's inadequate. For instance, to understand the metaphor we must ignore that factories have windows.

Shklovsky liked to mention the weather, the landscape, or some industrial or mechanical image from the streets. It was a convention to mention them, and he liked to use conventions, if only to draw attention to their conventionality. He used to insert, abruptly, material from his "time and place." In addition he would try to be succinct, although he was never in a hurry to get to his point.

Like anyone I also have a time and a place. Today I stopped to watch some men on Mission Street using a radial saw to cut into the sidewalk. As I walked home, up some cement stairs, I thought up a meaning for this image: "Everything we make we also have to unmake."

Ten years ago this unthinking factory began to process me. But what does that tell you? What can the written give you but a growing accumulation of detail?

Ten years ago it was my job to cook large pots of lentil soup in aluminum pots. Another job I had was to whip eggs in a machine called a Hobart. Books arrived in the mail once a week in the barn where I lived. They were my own OPOYAZ.

Ten years ago I started thinking a lot about the term "delay." I was trying to understand what kept a delay from collapsing in on itself. Of course it turned out to be time. I wrote my conclusion in a brown notebook.

Ten years before ten years ago I had some problems falling asleep. I kept trying to get a few things straight in my head. If time was a kind of processing something, then thinking seemed like a kind of chewing something.

I can hardly convey how desperately I wanted my thoughts to digest my confusion. But it's not always the case that a metaphor works. In reality, thoughts are not very effective chewers. At best they are like certain moths that die when you fondle them.

It's night now, with a clear sky. The freeway is almost silent. I think it's best to wrap up these notes in a few sentences.

Every articulation, I started to say, is sustained by its false hopes, its backward motions, and its disorderly pains from birth. Whether consciously or not, assertions are the living products of such ghosts.

Ordering and objectifying will always have this same problem. It will be haunted by a fourth factory, dreamlike, and nothing you do, even trying to be honest, even aiming directly at your intention, even framing the debate in whatever terms you value, will escape the physical picture of the unimaginable.

A person does wake up. And this can be used to prove that thought and language will, eventually, digest a person's doubts, since it is now morning.

But it can also prove the opposite. It can prove that a person will struggle and agonize until they stop trying to solve their life through words.

ANDREW JORON

A Season Later Than Winter

An empty spacesuit stands propped in a corner of the half-ruined Museum of Flight. This note was found clutched in its glove.

While seeds survive the winter, the flower that disseminated them does not. Likewise, the mind that understands this, and disseminates these words, will not survive the winter.

The line extends itself, the circle stands still.

I want to insist that the cycle of the seasons does not constitute a natural life-cycle: the analogy between the fate of a living organism and the Earth's orbital oscillation fails at the boundary between biological and mechanical motion, on the day of the longest night.

The swing of the pendulum represents not propagation but merely alternation. Unlike the alternator, the propagator never returns to an initial position. Once that light that inhabits fails, it fails with finality.

No doubt, the progress of spring, summer, fall, and winter corresponds to the birth, growth, senescence, and death of the organism. But the organism dies even as the world-clock is reset to zero. Here, the analogy between creature and creation breaks down.

Once this discontinuity is revealed, the passage from winter to spring can no longer be taken for granted. It assumes the power of contingency, the possibility of nothingness to become anything at all.

Here, the imagination wants to construct a new season, one capable of mediating between darkness and light. But let us avoid all mystical or religious fabulation, and imagine this undiscovered season as occurring within nature, as perhaps restoring a missing piece of nature.

How can time accommodate this moment that comes after the end, before the beginning? Only by moving sideways, like a line of writing.

MELISSA KWASNY

Learning to Speak with Them

Suppose you are walking in a place you have frequented enough to be stopped by the deep shaded green the blue spruce has turned in summer. Perhaps you even notice how it grows singular, unattended, unlike the Douglas fir and lodgepole pine that crowd the slopes above it, how it lives where it can soak its roots in the creek. You might even know this tree's name—Engelmann—and that it needs this unshared light around it. You stop. It is so beautiful. You want to draw it toward you. You'd like to know something of what it knows. Perhaps it could teach you how to live.

Should you kneel below it? Should you touch it, gaze up through its branches? Does it really matter how you approach it? Basho records how the peasants dressed in their finest to climb the mountain passes. The Cree here in Montana smudge themselves with smoking sweetgrass or cedar before they gather herbs. How to speak to it? Well, easy it is to speak. But you're not looking for ordinary speech as commerce, as Stephané Mallarmé writes, speech as "a commercial approach to reality."[1] You want something deeper, a communication, a communion.

One place to find a tradition of communicating with plants and animals, with the non-human (a phrase I will use instead of the word "nature") is in the oral poetry and transcribed songs of the Native American tribes:

How shall I begin my songs
In the blue night that is settling?

In the great night my heart will go out,
Toward me the darkness comes rattling.

In the great night my heart will go out.

In a traditional song such as this Papago "Owl Woman Song," what is immediately striking to me is the indeterminate nature of speaker and addressee. Who is speaking to whom? The speaker could be at once owl (personification), human becoming owl (metaphor), or human addressing owl (apostrophe), going out to meet its "darkness" halfway. Owl/woman: the poem enacts both realities at once—one speaks to the owl, yet, at the same time, one is speaking for it. Or rather, in order to speak for the owl, one must speak as it; the speaker, thus, is both transcriber of song and creator of song, both listener and singer.

Song of the Thunders

> Sometimes I
> Go about pitying
> Myself
> While I am carried by the wind
> Across the sky.[2]

Though transcribed from their native languages by the ethnomusicologist Frances Densmore only two or three generations ago, these songs, given to the singer through the spirit of the plant or animal, seem ancient. They seem to belong not only to another people, but to another world, a world that was not, we are taught, real. "Before I came on this world," said the Crow medicine woman Pretty Shield to Frank B. Linderman in 1932, "and even for a time afterward, my people saw strange things, heard words spoken that they did not always understand. Now, they see nothing, hear nothing that is strange."[3]

This strangeness, this sense of being able to transverse worlds, is an aim we see again and again in poem-making. The desire to disperse or de-center the self evidenced in many contemporary texts is part of a larger tradition that can be traced back to poetry's origins in prayer, prophesy and spell. What poets are importantly interested in: when another voice takes over. What we name that voice-the muse of the Greeks, the Holy Imagination of the romantics, the unconscious of the surrealists, the duendé of Andalusian flamenco singers, the Other of post-colonial discourse-of course, has fluctuated. And yet, as André Breton writes, "we still know as little as we ever did about the origin of the voice which it is everyone's prerogative to hear, if only he will, a voice which converses with us most specifically about something other than what we believe we are thinking."4

When we use the word voice in regard to poetry, we usually mean the voice the poet speaks with, though that voice can be dispersed across different figures within the text. Voice usually includes choices in diction, syntax, rhythm, and image. Yet, how does the world speak to us? What voices do we hear, as opposed to speak with? And how is a translation made?

What I have learned from the traditional Native people here in Montana is that the songs one sings in the ceremonies are owned by the singer. One can ask for someone else's song, but only by going through the proper rituals. One can never buy a song. Initially, a song must be given by the spirit of the being one contacts, whether that being is the eagle, the aspen, the sky or the earth, such as in this description of a young man's vision quest by the Sioux spiritual leader Black Elk: "He must be careful less distracting thoughts come to him, yet he must be alert to recognizing any messenger which the Great Spirit may send him for these people often come in the form of an animal, even one as small and as seemingly insignificant as the little ant."5 Through fasting, prayer and ritual purification, the seeker was able to commune with the non-human and transform that communion into language, into an art form he or she could use. Once a song is made, it unites both singer and spirit. If one continues to sing and then neglects the source of that song, at best the spirit will leave the singer; at worst it could drive her mad. In other words, the making of a song proposes a path, a relationship.

Oread

> Whirl up, sea,
> whirl your pointed pines,
> splash your great pines
> on our rocks,
> hurl your green over us,
> cover us with your pools of fir.[6]

In his working papers, the poet George Oppen writes that he could never have written a poem such as H.D.'s "Oread;" he could never think to command the sea.[7] Whether it is the sea that is addressed or the sea of trees which make up the forest covering the mountains in Pennsylvania, where H.D. grew up, a wooded slope incipient with wind, is disputable. An oread is a mountain spirit. Is the poet then adopting the persona of the spirit of the mountain commanding its forces? Or is the speaker a woman conjuring—rather than commanding—the mountain spirit, in this case its manifestation as wind? The poem has the purposefulness of a spell, of something set in motion by the act of its being spoken. Conjure: to summon in a sacred name, to enjoin. As in the Native American examples before it, there is, in "Oread," an indeterminacy of speaker and addressee, a voice shift flickering back and forth between the you and I. One might call it multiple subjectivity. One might also call it what Sufi scholar Henri Corbin names, in his discussion of the creative imagination, "a dialogical situation."[8]

It would be helpful here to look at the term "creative imagination" and to try to separate it from the diminished meaning with which we have come to regard the imaginary—as fantasy, unreality, un-tethered association, a simile-making machine. Ralph Waldo Emerson uses the term "active imagination" in his essay "The Poet," and defines it as "a very high sort of seeing, which does not come by study, but by the intellect being where and what it sees; by sharing the path or circuit of things through forms, and so making them translucid to others."[9]

H.D.'s method speaks of a similar translation through forms. "We begin with sympathy of thought," she writes in *Notes on Thought and Vision*, a book-length essay in which she explains her method of generating images as an action described in the figure of a jelly fish: "When the center of consciousness and the jelly-fish is in the body, (I visualize it in my case lying on the left side with streamers or feelers floating up toward the brain) we have vision of the womb or love-vision."[10] The imagination, in this case, is conceived as an act rather than a quality or description (as in imaginary), as a movement out from the body and toward its subject, whether the thought of the subject or the existence of the subject itself.

H.D. uses the precision she learned in her early Imagist practice to describe the wind in trees for us. At the same time, she conjures a mythological and/or hermetic being, a figure "entering the imagination,' according to Adelaide Morris, "from another dimension and carrying with [it] the mysterious radiance by which H.D. gratefully remapped our 'dead, old, thousand times explored old world.'"[11] Yet, the subject of H.D.'s poem is not only the oread, I would argue, despite its Greek title. Could the poem not at the same time be read as adopting a voice which co-exists with us here on earth and yet is other-the wind, the trees, the wind-in-the-trees?

This dual life—the image as both earthly presence and symbolic presence, as both literal and figurative, concrete and abstract—is something one recognizes in the Native American examples. At the same time that there is a particular owl being addressed, there is the sense of owl as representation or earthly manifestation of Owl People. How then do these exist at the same time and how are both existences quickened when the poem/song is spoken/sung? In his book *Creative Imagination in the Sufism of Ibn Arabi*, Corbin uses the term "creative imagination" or theophonic prayer to describe a technique employed by the Sufi mystics in ancient Iran.[12] It is a practice the Sufis used to visualize, and thus meet, the god-head, a method perhaps akin to H.D.'s. The practice depended on the positing of a three-fold vision of the world:

The World of Mystery
*
The World of Pure Images
*
The World of Our Senses

    Between the World of Mystery, to which we have no direct access and the concrete world perceivable by our five senses is what Corbin calls the "*mundus imaginalis*," an imaginal realm.[13] The creative imagination, he states, functions as an "intermediary, a mediatrix,"[14] between these worlds. It shares, as Emerson states, "a path or circuit of things through forms." That circuit is the flicker between symbolic and concrete we often feel in any precisely rendered image. How explain it? "The unity of being conditions the dialogical situation," Corbin writes. The Sufis did not "make things up" out of thin air. Their visions came in the forms of earthly things, in flowers, rivers, fountains, birds, animals, light.

    If I substitute the word "being" or "life" for "The World of Mystery," I can find a way of thinking about the image and its use, at least in poetry, as a means of communication with the non-human. In many ways, our distrust of the symbol is a question of hermeneutics, of who or what gets to interpret the image. This is why the work of Corbin is instructive. The Sufis were not adherents of clerical Islam. They believed in their visions, not because the visions reaffirmed an ecclesiastical interpretation, but because they had created them, they had brought them into being in a form they could see and understand. Corbin says that the mystics, as differentiated from those who practiced the official religion of Islam, were after an individual, ephiphanic experience. The goal of the "visualizations" (a practice so complex, hermetic and committed that I do not pretend to understand it) was to meet with one's own personal manifestation of the divine. The power to create was granted by one's belief in the possibility of communion, a highly individualized communion in which the mystic and the god take part, a two-fold meeting for which both sides are responsible.

The question, though, for me remains: Is the rendering of precise image a form of attention to this world or a means of departure from it? Is the non-human another dimension we have been excluding or is the non-human a symbol masking a mystical or symbolic dimension, an other than earthly dimension? Do animals and plants stand for something else, and thus, lose their value as beings that exist? Are they not things in themselves, rich with knowledge of what it means to live on this earth, knowledge which is not ours? Is not the 'natural object," as Pound writes, ". . . the adequate symbol?"[15]

The Sea Rose

> Rose, harsh rose,
> marred and with stint of petals,
> meager flower, thin,
> sparse of leaf,
>
> more precious
> than a wet rose
> single on a stem—
> you are caught in the drift. [16]

It is obvious that the sea rose in the above poem is a concrete, individual rose, that H.D. has seen it, is perhaps seeing it as she writes, that she is perhaps writing au plein-air as painters do. The image is precise and lean, a perfect example of an early Imagist poem, which Pound defined as "austere, direct, free from emotional slither."[17] But, though one of the aims of Imagism was to avoid solipsism, to let the image speak for itself without imposing meaning from without (cultural, historical, religious) and from within (the unconscious), H.D. also knew her Greek mythology, was conversant in hermetic lore; she was, as well, a student of Freud's. In this poem, the rose, a figure fraught with symbolic meaning, is described concretely. Yet, because the poem is countering the old symbologies of rose—this rose is harsh, not lovely; marred, not perfect; stinted, not voluptuous, beleaguered in the wild, not safe in a bouquet—it, too, begins to reflect a symbolic reality, even a subversive one. One does not think of a rose as "marred," "meager," "sparse." She tells us it is more precious. Why? Is it because it survives past our stereotypes of rose? Is it because it survives at all? And who, again, is speaking? The rose is addressed as a you. Personification? Or is the poet "like" a rose, feeling stunted and flung about by the forces of the world? Or is she both, enacting the "dialogical situation" Corbin speaks of, the voice as both rose and poet?

 The Wild Iris, Louise Gluck's lyrically beautiful book-length sequence of poems, continues the tradition of H.D.'s early Imagist poems by employing keen and precise observation in its attention to the non-human world. The poems take as their point of attention the flowers in Gluck's summer and end-of-summer garden: the wild iris, trillium, poppies, clover, violets. The book begins with the title poem:

> At the end of my suffering
> there was a door.
>
> Hear me out: that which you call death
> I remember.
>
> Overhead, noises, branches of the pine shifting.
> Then nothing. The weak sun
> flickered over the dry surface. [18]

At first glance, we assume that the iris is speaking; we might even sense the voice as a kind of conceit, a personification or instance of anthropomorphism, the iris as mask for the speaker. There is an "I" which is attempting to describe what happens when we die and what it might mean to live again. There is a "you" to whom this lesson is taught. The "you" has a word for the end of life—death—and so must be human. Yet, as in the previous poems, the speaker—and the poems almost always use first person point of view-is indeterminate, often mysteriously. Does an iris "suffer?" And if the iris has died back at the end of its season, who then is describing "the weak sun?" It must be someone still here, someone who has also the word "door," who can still hear overhead the shifting of birds. It is as if the point of view had changed from plant to observer of plant, as if the speaker is both inside the experience and outside it, is a flower who suffers and one who can recognize an end to suffering, as if, as the poet Clayton Eshleman writes in *Juniper Fuse*, his mediation on the origin of images, "seeing into and seeing through combined into a winding window." [19]

The vegetative world gives literal evidence of the cycle of death and regeneration. An iris bulb, especially, which propagates by bulb and is perennial, will return each spring to the spot it has died back to. Flowers, for this reason, have heavy truck in our tradition as religious symbols of rebirth and redemption after suffering, of the spirit's winter and spring, night and dawn. The poem ends, "whatever / returns from oblivion returns / to find a voice: / from the center of my life came / a great fountain, deep blue / shadows on azure seawater." The speaker is resurrected not as a voice, but an image. Flowers are the most silent of things. Their voice comes to us in shape and color. Gluck identifies the speaker not as iris, but as "consciousness." But whose? Identity flickers as the sun does on the dry ground from flower to human to a widely dispersed god as gardener, or gardener as god. The image of a fountain might refer to the god of the Old Testament. Or it could be Orpheus who suffered the grief of love, descended to the underworld and came up singing. Or it could be Jesus who blossomed out of his cave.

In some poems, the voice is clearly human—"Noah says this is / an error of depressives, identifying with a tree"—in some, that of a flower—"The great thing / is not having / a mind"—or that of the gardener-god speaking to the plants—"You wanted to be born; I let you be born." However, the majority of the poems trade between dual, or triple, identities. In "Trillium," the speaker wakes in the forest and we are not sure if it is the yellow flower or the poet who is waking.

When Ezra Pound states in his Imagist manifesto that "the natural object is always the adequate symbol," one could read the statement as an attempt to grant the world its autonomy, in effect, to grant the non-human world its voice. Pound uses the term phanopoeia to describe "the casting of images upon the visual imagination of the reader, crediting the early Chinese poets as being adept at this. "In phanopoeia," he writes, "we find the greatest drive toward precision of the word."[20] However, Gluck's flowers are not only precisely described; they speak. They speak not only of the biological life cycle of a flower, but of redemption, atonement, resurrection, belief and disbelief, all notions deeply connotative of a Judeo/Christian tradition. Seven poems are entitled "Matins" and ten "Vespers." Many address a god in Western patriarchal terms: "Unreachable father." The natural object as adequate symbol? The phrase seems a paradoxical one. Is it possible to see the thing itself?

The confusion, it seems to me, can be located in the nature of the symbol itself. The natural object as symbol of what? When Charles Baudelaire writes, in his famous poem "Correspondences" that "man passes through forests of symbols / Which observe him with familiar eyes,"[21] he is speaking to the "doctrine of correspondences," a doctrine posited by 18th century mystic Emanuel Swedenborg who believed, like the Sufi mystics Corbin studied, that the sensory world is a reflection of a parallel corresponding world of spirit. In fact, one of the tenets of French symbolism—whose adherents were familiar with the writings of Swedenborg—was a profound belief that the world speaks to us. I have often wondered if the *haunting objects*[22] that permeated the imaginations of the romantics and symbolists—the rose, the swan, the albatross—are so very different in function from the haunting objects of the tribal people in America—the eagle, the bear, the water panther. Yet, there are profound differences. Because, before symbolism—and I am speaking here of the symbolism for which Mallarmé was spokesman—the nature of an object was assigned to a meaning bound to one's time and culture, however circumscribed or open-ended, whether tribal, Christian, Hindu, Eastern, Western. Each symbol is created, maintained, and interpreted in light of generations of stories and songs that come down through cultural history. To let go the rein of traditional hermeneutics was one of the aims of the symbolist movement, to free the image so it could be free-floating, un-interpreted, and thus, remain numinous, maintaining its own life as object. Mallarmé recognized the power in certain images and yet, he felt that to explain or describe them robs them of their mystery: "It is not description which can unveil the efficacy and beauty of monuments, seas, or the human face in all their maturity and native state, but rather evocation, *allusion, suggestion.*"[23] Mallarmé was not interested in nailing down the lid on the coffin of meaning, but of evoking the mysteries of existence. His ideal poem would allow the concrete object to suggest its symbolic reality, if only for us to feel, never interpret, the life-force behind it.

According to *The New Princeton Encyclopedia of Poetry and Poetics*, Mallarmé believed that "the creation of the symbol occurs in two ways: a haunting object permeates little by little the consciousness of the poet and is associated with a state of being of which the poet was not initially aware. The other direction of the image/mood association is from the inside outward: a state of being or an unnamable feeling is projected onto an exterior world, targeting an object or landscape which gives it embodiment."[24] What is key here is that the symbol is "created." It is made by the intersession of the concrete object and the gazing subject; in terms of this essay, between the non-human and the poet. What is the nature of that intersession? Mallarmé does not differentiate between the two methods of creating the symbol, whether from attention to something that calls to the poet or whether from the poet departing from herself toward her object. According to Corbin, it is the same for the Sufi mystics: "To say that one of our thoughts, sentiments, or desires is concretized in a form specific to the intermediate plane of Idea-Images of subtile matter is the same as to meditate before a flower, a mountain or a constellation in order to discover not what obscure and unconscious force they manifest, but what divine thought, flowering in the world of spirit, is epiphanized, is at work in them."[25]

Mallarmé was only mildly interested in the concrete object, the real swan or deer in the forest. The object existed only as doorway to symbolic encounter, and, once passed through, lost its necessity and, quite properly, should disappear: "Why should we perform the miracle by which a natural object is almost made to disappear beneath the magic waving wand of the written word, if not to divorce that object from the direct and the palpable, and so conjure up its *essence* in all purity."[26] Can we have both the direct and palpable, which Mallarmé denounces, along with "the forest's shuddering," which he advocates for? Can we respect both the concrete and symbolic reality of the forms of life before us? Can poetry do this, enact what is essentially a transference, a communion with another without weighing the encounter down with outworn symbologies, leaving the interpretation of the image up for grabs, or vacating the object altogether? The danger of a poetics of attention is that we will project our desires onto the object, that in our departure we return to the self or culture we were trying to escape.

> In the small beauty of the forest
> The wild deer bedding down—
> That they are there! [27]

In George Oppen's well-known poem "Psalm," the first stanza asserts the right of the deers to exist in themselves and not as symbols. The poet sees and praises the fact of the deers' presence with Imagist precision, detailing the roots which "dangle from their mouths / scattering earth in the strange woods" and how "their alien small teeth / tear at the grass." How astonishing, the poet seems to be saying. "They who are there," he repeats, who are there and not us. Oppen seems intent on seeing only what is, in its thingness, to find words, simple words arranged in a way that would "construct meaning," that would awaken us to the reality of our existence on earth. "If we were born, full blown, in space," he writes in one of his daybooks, "a planet hanging enormously in front of us, no one would hunt for misty words or for 'mysticism.' One would say look! Or, do you see it? Or What is it? I should suppose that nothing—nothing at all—but the constant repetition of abstract words could blind us to that presence." [28]

> The small nouns
> Crying faith
> In this in which the wild deer
> Startle, and stare out.

There are, of course, many ways to read this poem—and many contemporary schools of poetics have claimed Oppen for their own. Yet, most would agree that part of his project is to render experience objectively, to attend to it without symbol or decoration, to attend without self-regard or self-mystification. Oppen's "Psalm" makes no large claims; it is a "small" beauty that is going to be described. He will use "small" nouns in order to do this. He will try to get out of the way.

Any naming is evidence of a desire for an encounter, of a "faith" that words will draw us closer. Unlike H.D., Oppen would never presume to speak for the deer. He does, however, speak to the distance that divides them. After all, are the woods "strange" to Oppen or to the deer? Are their teeth "alien" to him or to the grass? Do the words he uses to describe this experience—his own experience of it—separate him or bring him closer? Oppen is astonished that the deer are there, yet implicit in his statement is the fact that he is also astonished that we are. Because of the acute attention Oppen pays not only to the deer but to his experience of *meeting* the deer, there is, as in the many poems cited, a moment where we can feel that meeting as it might feel from both sides: hesitant, quiet, careful, startled. The deer stares out of its particular world as Oppen stares out of his. One is startled that another world exists beyond the self. This startling is a perception of difference that both deer and person share. How does the poem manage this transference? With respect, Oppen might answer, as he does in another poem, "The Hills," with respect and a conviction to honor the other in its other life, to attend, to be present in that meeting:

> That this is I,
> Not mine, which wakes
> To where the present
> Sun pours in the present, to the air perhaps
> Of love and of
> Conviction. [29]

Much contemporary poetry, as well as the means used to construct it—occlusion, omission, elision—avoids interpreting the image or connecting strings of images, letting, as Mallarmé would say, the silences speak. What might be found in those silences? One of the reasons I have been stressing the image when, paradoxically, I am writing about communication, is because obviously we do not share a language with non-human forms of life. "The paths of things are silent," Emerson writes. "Will they suffer a speaker to go with them? A spy they will not suffer; a lover, a poet, is the transcendency of their own nature."[30] In a world that seems increasingly focused on the needs of humans, when plants and animals are dying out at an alarming rate, the struggle to widen the world to one where we exist in relation to other forms of life seems crucial. Examining the ways poets both "read" and render that relation might help us effect a transcendency of our own.

1. Mallarmé, Stephané. "Crisis in Poetry" in *Mallarmé: Selected Prose Poems, Essays,& Letters.* Baltimore: John Hopkins Press, 1956, p. 40.

2. Both poems are from *The Sky Clears: Poetry of the American Indians*, edited by A. Grove Day. Lincoln: University of Nebraska Press, 1951. The translations are by Frances Densmore.

3. Linderman, Frank B. *Pretty-Shield: Medicine Woman of the Crows.* Lincoln: University of Nebraska Press, 1972, p. 126.

4. Breton, André. "Second Manifesto of Surrealism" in *Manifestoes of Surrealism.* Richard Seaver and Helen R. Lane, translators. Ann Arbor: University of Michigan Press, 1972, p. 158.

5. Brown, Joseph Epes. *The Sacred Pipe: Black Elk's Account of the Seven Rites of the Oglala Sioux.* Norman: University of Oklahoma press, 1953, p. 58.

6. H.D. *Collected Poems: 1912-1944.* New York: New Directions, 1983, p. 55.

7. Oppen, George. "An Adequate Vision: From the Daybooks." Michael Davidson, editor. *Ironwood*, 1982, p. 9.

8. Corbin, Henri. *Creative Imagination in the Sufism of Ibn Arabi.* Princeton: Princeton University Press, 1981, p. 247.

9. Emerson, Ralph Waldo. "The Poet," in *The Selected Writings of Ralph Waldo Emerson.* New York: Modern Library, 1992, p. 298.

10. H.D. *Notes on Thought and Vision.* San Francisco: City Lights, 1982, p. 20.

11. Morris, Adelaide. "The Concept of Projection: H.D.'s Visionary Powers," in *Signets*, Rachel Blau DuPlessis and Susan Friedman, editors. Madison: University of Wisconsin Press, 1981, p. 282.

12. Corbin. *Creative Imagination*, p. 264.

13. Corbin, Henri. *The Man of Light in Iranian Sufism.* New Lebanon, New York: Omega Publications, 1994, p. 16.

14. Corbin. *Creative Imagination*, p. 217.

15. Pound, Ezra. "A Retrospect" in *Literary Essays of Ezra Pound.* New York: New Directions, 1935, p. 5.

16. H.D. *Collected Poems*, p. 5.

17. Pound, p. 12.

18. Gluck, Louise. *The Wild Iris*. Hopewell: Ecco Press, p. 1.

19. Eshleman, Clayton. *Juniper Fuse: Upper Paleothic Imagination and the Construction of the Underworld*. Middletown: Wesleyan University press, p. xxii.

20. Pound, p. 26.

21. Baudelaire, Charles. *Selected Poems*. Wallace Fowlie, trans. New York: Dover, p. 5.

22. Preminger, Alex and T.V.F. Brogan, editors. *The New Princeton Encyclopedia of Poetry and Poetics*. Princeton: Princeton University Press, 1999, p. 11256.

23. Mallarmé, p. 40.

24. *The New Princeton Encyclopedia*, p. 1256.

25. Corbin. *Creative Imagination*, p. 236.

26. Mallarmé, p. 42.

27. Oppen, George. *The Collected Poems of George Oppen*. New York: New Directions, 1975, p. 78.

28. Oppen, George. *George Oppen's Working Papers*, edited with an Introduction by Stephen Cope. *The Germ*, 4. Santa Cruz. The Poetic Research Bloc (May 1999).

29. Oppen. *Collected*, p. 54.

30. Emerson, p. 298.

ANDREW JORON

On Negative Lyric

Any critical, experimentally realist, lyric, to the extent that it refuses to reproduce what is, must be committed to the creation of what isn't. This anti-mimetic imperative will cause the lyric finally to overflow the bounds of its critical (socially responsible) mandate. Within experimental lyric, the critical moment (predicated on a given reality) and the creative moment (which yields a new reality) exist together, in tension. Yet the former holds as its regulative principle an uncoerced condition of being, and the latter—through its inevitable violation of peaceful equilibrium—an unreconciled one. The critical moment is mediated by a vision of social justice, whereas the creative moment is—in an important sense—unmediated, inasmuch as it is motivated by the immediacy of its encounter with an un(re)cognizable Otherness.

These principles appear to diverge precisely at the crux between language and the body. Experimental lyric stages its resistance to the dominant ideology, not merely through the presentation of competing ideas, but through the invention of "a new sensorium," one whose pulsions and intensities cannot be conducted on the level of conventional language. Lyric songfulness (even redefined as the singing of song's impossibility) overflows the concept by working on the non-conceptual infrastructure of thought—in others words, by reawakening the body.

The body, with its disequilibriating flows of desire, never completely succumbs to the taming and disciplining of culture—whereas language, at least in everyday practice, tends to serve as the instrument of domination. Consequently, lyric poets since Romanticism have turned to the convulsive "mind" of the body as an agency for guiding language out of the reified lifeworld. The challenge of the experimental lyric, then, is the re-embodiment of the word—no longer with the aim, as in some versions of Romanticism, of restoring a lost totality, but in order to manifest, through a de-naturalized and even de-anthropomorphized sensorium, the non-totalizable sublimity of the real.

Ultimately, the lyric will realize itself by drawing upon and releasing the energies of self-organizing processes occurring at levels of material interaction beyond intentionality. "Language," as the founding Language poets always emphasized, "knows more than we do"—but so does the body, as the Surrealists insisted. An experimentally lyrical practice, therefore, must prove capable of opening itself to the Otherness of those modalities (both bodily and linguistic) that exceed the social project even as they materially transform it.

The incorporation of such apocalyptic (even messianic) moments into poetry would hardly be countenanced by even so radical a critic as Adorno (who preferred to uphold the power of the negative as intervallic suspension rather than as irruptive alterity). For critical realism, the question comes down to: How should the poem give voice to suffering, which according to Adorno is the precondition of truth? Today, it is barbaric, not just to forget suffering, but also to preserve it in a crystal of "never forgetting" (which could only reify it); the lyric imperative here, instead, is to move with suffering, tracing its cry against its own condition in the form of an opening toward something other than itself: Utopia.

(From a Notebook)

Good quote from the painter John Button on seeing a particular Bonnard: "Sometimes I think that Bonnard is the culmination of twentieth century art. I was recently taken to the house of a collector ... over the mantle a Bonnard, certainly the finest I've seen. Everything about the painting was wonderful . . . what makes it good? Who knows. The incredible surface, the astonishing color, the light that pours out of it, or the feeling in it . . . Bonnard seems to have looked at the little breakfast table and its window, *fixed his heart on all of life*, and painted." (My italics.)

A woman behind me says to her friend, "look what my hand just fell on."

A baby just dropped her plastic bottle of formula SMACK onto the floor.

As someone who occasionally writes in equal stanzas, I'm susceptible to some goofy vibrations about some of them. Quatrains, for example, have a vibe completely different from any other stanza. They're good conveyors of a well-formed kind of thought, but they can also put thought into a kind of jail. (Dickinson: Erectrix of exquisite jail.) Even when the statement is going on past the boundaries of the individual quatrain there's a boxiness there that is ambiguous: it can add fiber, but also starch. I never sense this in couplets or tercets-they're better with a looser, more fluid thought, even when they wholly contain it. It might be the four-corner feeling in the quatrain, the foundation of which veers away from "nature," and toward architecture.

Film situation: 1962, or thereabouts.A young couple, with a youngster in tow (a five or six-year-old), staying at a run-down motel for an extended time. Somewhere out west and remote (off an old highway in Nevada, say).They're not on vacation, and there's nothing holiday-like about about the place, which has a drained pool and almost no other inhabitants. Why are they there? Are they handing the kid over to a foster family in a week? Or waiting to hear about tests from a nearby hospital that is putting them up at the motel? Whatever the reason is, it should come out very gradually and slowly. The real film is simply observing these three, the boy off doing things by himself to pass the time (playing in the drained pool, etc.), the couple together, passing the time, trying to make love at night while the boy is asleep, sometimes arguing, etc. Sometimes each is alone with the boy. There should be a shadow of anxiety — and the fear of loss — over the situation, since they are not there by choice (but again, the reason should be disclosed very gradually, in stages).The couple are attractive and competent enough, though maybe attractive mostly because they're young. He is close to six feet, lean, trying to keep things together. He wears khakis and a tee-shirt, and khaki shorts if it's warm. If they leave the motel to go some-where, he'll put on a short-sleeved shirt. She is maybe 5' 6", maybe strawberry-blonde, usually in a blouse and slacks, but really likes sum-mer dresses and wears them occasionally (though with no occasion). The boy is small, skinny, and quiet as hell. He's a tow-head, but buzzed. He is rarely bored and almost never complains, being able to entertain himself for the most part (the drained pool is a great play-ground).And there they are, these three, waiting for a day in the next week, a day of answered prayer or worst wish. Young, resilient, but inexperienced and in over their heads.

Rereading all of Lew Welch recently—the "Ring of Bone" volume—I was struck by how consistently good it is, how high the quality, how clean the vision. When he was on, he really knew how to sound his thought. The unfinished or unpublished work at the back of the book shows that he also knew how to select—he is unerring about the less-realized work. I actually like the idea of a short collected poems, but in Welch's case it wasn't an "idea" but bad forces that kept it short. My used copy of "Ring of Bone" has a faded news clipping from the *Chronicle* tucked into it, with the rending headline: POET HUNT ENDS.

The baby drops her formula again WHACK. This time I look up and there's someone on a unicycle passing quickly past the window, while the bass rumble of a hip-hop convertible—the kind with the massive woofer in the back seat-starts to be heard from, what, two blocks away, just as I catch sight of a woman in a stunning print dress in a corner of the café, reading Badiou. It's one of those moments of near-simultaneous random input from crazily disparate sources, an unprovoked and unprotected NOW that brings you to the bald surface of time, part epiphany and part punch-line. Or, as Frank O'Hara says, "Everything suddenly honks." What was it in the poem? 2:10 of a Tuesday? (Actually, it was "12:40 of a Thursday," I now see, back at the flat.) "A Step Away from Them." A sort of companion-poem to "The Day Lady Died," and I think an equally great one. In both, the poet is "walking in New York" if not standing still, on his lunch hour, a flâneur on a work schedule. In each, his stroll is interrupted: in one, by a stark headline and photo in the *New York Post*; in the other, by a darker musing about loss and the uncertain nature of mortality. "The Day Lady Died" ends with O'Hara seeing the news of Billie Holiday's death and remembering the electric moment when she sang a few impromptu numbers in the Five Spot tavern, accompanied by pianist Mal Waldron. She was courting arrest by doing so, since she'd had her cabaret card revoked (a heroin conviction), and thus in these circumstances could be put in jail for committing song. One can scarcely imagine the charge of being that must have crackled through those privileged few minutes, of witnessing and experiencing a great artist's defiance through her art. O'Hara doesn't attempt to reconstruct, saying only that "everyone and I stopped breathing." In poems like these,

George Albon **249**

all one's qualms about O'Hara's immersion in the heroics of culture are swept aside. Giants really were allowed to walk the earth in those days, and devotion to the furthest and newest reaches in the arts, "high" or popular, was construed as true oppositionality. Such a thing hadn't quite yet lost its aura of holy, indigent vocation. At the same time culture was the maypole around which one's life and one's friends' and lovers' lives revolved, both reverence *and* play. Art may not have been more important than life, but "at times when I would rather be dead the thought that I could never write another poem has so far stopped me."

"The roar of memory"—Ginsberg / "The soil's roar"—Niedecker

"A Step Away From Them" also chronicles an hour or so of everyday life which is brought up short, but in this poem there has been a somber reflection, rather than news received, in the midst of walking life. It's a more ambiguous poem, and the ambiguity begins with the title. A step away from them—but is that a short step or a long one? Is "away" time or space? If it's time, he will be following them soon enough. If it's space, his remaining in life has put him at one remove, even from those whose loss he will never truly absorb. This step is a full step; in the first reading, it's a mere one. But of course it's both. According to Brad Gooch's biography, O'Hara wrote it the day after Jackson Pollock's funeral, and so thoughts of loss and absence must have been, amid the grand chaos of midtown Manhattan, unavoidably sounding. The poem recalls the music of Francis Poulenc (a passion of O'Hara) in which a carefree surface will suddenly give way to unexpected depths of melancholy. It's a classic "I do this, I do that" poem, O'Hara digging his lunch hour-shopping for a wristwatch, noticing the laborers and Puerto Ricans on the avenue, admiring the daylight neon. Then toward the close, there's a sudden meditation on artists (and friends) who have passed ("First / Bunny died, then John Latouche, / then Jackson Pollock"), and then a strangely phrased wondering ("But is the / earth as full as life was full, of them?"). The word "earth" could intend something like "grave" but also something like "our world without them," that is, their legacy (and effect) among the living. The question is casually put, but steeply considered. Everyone who knew O'Hara well testifies to his gift for friendship; it came as naturally to him as breathing. I attended a reading of Robert Glück a few years back, and he prefaced the work he was going to read by saying that it was occasioned by the effect of friendship on the imagination. This is also O'Hara's world. And it was inextricable from artistic purpose: a friend was someone to bounce ideas off, to collaborate with, to goad, to write about, to love the works of. At the same time, O'Hara and his friends are moving into a time of life that is decidedly past youth's natural carapace, away from its breezy resilience, and into a period when abrasions—deaths, estrangements, even the calculus of new relationships—linger a bit longer than they used to. His work from this point on loses some of its aestheticized veneer and becomes looser, both more documentary and more multivocal, in its approach. The fleeting moment is more likely to nudge its way in, as if seeking parity with the "poetic," just as the poetry will continue to commune in the company of those no longer alive but still in life. "A glass of papaya juice / and back to work. My heart is in my / pocket, it is Poems by Pierre Reverdy." Thus ends the poem. It's a common juncture for him, of death-awareness, of the permeability of death-in-life, and of the symbiosis of life, friendship, and art. It's at this point that O'Hara, the genius of protean circumstance, and with some time left, moves back out onto the world's sidewalk.

I'll close this digression with an anecdote. Years ago, I was working at a large chain record store down from North Beach. It was a very busy place, chronically understaffed, with a bank of four cash registers on the main floor and a never-ending line of customers filing through. During one of my register shifts, a tweedy senior citizen brought up some CDs to buy (Chabrier, I think). "You used to have some small

CD crates," he said. "We're out of those," I replied, as I rang him up. (The customer-service philosophy at this place was "move-'em-through.") I punched the total, and he gave me a credit card. I glanced at the name: DONALD M ALLEN. "Are you Donald Allen the editor?" I asked. He gave me a look that seemed to be amusement but could have been other things. "How did you know that?" he asked. At that point I shifted into mild fandom: telling him how important his work as an editor was to me, how *The New American Poetry* was a revolutionary moment in literary history, and finally finishing up a minute later with ". . . in fact, *The Collected Poems of Frank O'Hara* was my highschool graduation present!" He paused for a second. Then asked, in a time-wasted tone of voice, "When do you suppose you might get some more of those crates?"

CONTRIBUTORS

Poet, performer, and interdisciplinary artist **DAVID ABEL** makes his living as a freelance editor and a bookseller in Portland, Oregon. Publications include the chapbooks *Black Valentine* (Chax Press, 2006) and *Cut* (Situations, 1999), and the artist's books and text objects *Threnos* (Katherine Kuehn, 2001), *Rose* (Salient Seedling, 1997), and *Selected Durations* (Salient Seedling, 1994). Recent performances and installations include "Tomorrow, Tomorrow, I Will Be Here Tomorrow" (4th Annual Richard Foreman Festival, Portland, 2006; with Anna Daedalus); *Eclipse* (Light and Sound Gallery, Portland, 2006; with John Berendzen); *Closet Drama* (Tucson, 2006); and *Signs in Situ* (The Land/an art site, Mountainair, NM, 2005; with Paul Maurer).

GEORGE ALBON's most recent book is *Step*, from Post-Apollo. He would like to recommend the following two books: *Betraying Spinoza* by Rebecca Goldstein, and *Why Arendt Matters* by Elisabeth Young-Bruehl. He lives in San Francisco.

RAE ARMANTROUT's most recent books are *Next Life* (Wesleyan, 2007) and *Up to Speed* (Wesleyan, 2004). She teaches writing and literature at the University of California San Diego.

MARY BURGER is the author of *Sonny* (Leon Works). She's a co-editor of *Biting the Error: Writers Explore Narrative*, and the editor of Second Story Books, featuring works of experimental narrative. *An Apparent Event: A Second Story Books Anthology* was published in 2006.

THOMAS A. CLARK was born in Greenock, Scotland in 1944. He and artist Laurie Clark started Moschatel Press in 1973. From 1986-2002 they ran the Cairn Gallery which specialized in Land Art, Minimalism, and lyric or poetic conceptualism. Recent publications include *One Hundred Scottish Places* (Eindhoven, Holland 1999) and *Distance & Proximity* (Pocket Books, Edinburgh 2001).

KATE COLBY grew up in Massachusetts and lives in San Francisco, where she works as a copywriter and editor. She is the author of *Fruitlands* (Litmus Press, 2006) and *Rock of Ages* (Anadama Press chapbook, 2005). Recent work can be found in *Bay Poetics, Parthenon West* and *Vanitas*.

BRENT CUNNINGHAM is a writer, publisher and visual artist living in Oakland, California. Since 1999 he has worked for Small Press Distribution (SPD) in Berkeley, and has served on the board of Small Press Traffic in San Francisco since 2001. His first book, *Bird & Forest*, was published by Ugly Duckling Presse in 2005. Links to more of his writing as well as much of his artwork can be found at brentcunningham.blogspot.com. Last year he and Neil Alger founded Hooke Press (hookepress.com), a chapbook press dedicated to publishing short runs of poetry, criticism, theory, writing and ephemera.

STEFFI DREWES lives in Oakland, CA. Her poems have appeared in *Shampoo, Traffic, Mirage*, and *Beeswax Magazine.*

ELISE FICARRA lives and works in San Francisco and is an affiliate artist at the Headlands Center for the Arts. Her book, *Swelter*, was winner of the Michael Rubin Chapbook Award in 2005. Her poetry has appeared in *Bird Dog, Dusie, Commonweal, Fourteen Hills, Parthenon West* and other journals. She is the business manager of The Poetry Center at SFSU.

PETER GURNIS also has a serial poem in the current issue of *First Intensity*, which along with "Holy Flight of Letters" is part of his book-length poem "Berlin and Eden." In 2005 he received a grant from the Howard Foundation to help him complete the project.

KRISTEN HANLON's chapbook *Proximity Talks* is available from Noemi Press.

ANTHONY HAWLEY is the author of *The Concerto Form* (Shearsman Books, 2006) and the chapbooks *Vocative* (Phylum Press, 2004) and *Afield* (Ugly Duckling Presse, 2004). Recent poems have appeared and are forthcoming in *Colorado Review, Denver Quarterly, Jacket, P-Queue*, and *Verse.*

ANDREW JORON is a poet, essayist, and translator. His most recent books are *Fathom* (Black Square Editions, 2003) and *The Cry at Zero: Selected Prose* (Counterpath Press, 2007).

ERICA KAUFMAN co-curates the belladonna* small press and reading series. She is the author of the chapbooks: *a familiar album, censory impulse, and the kickboxer suite.* Her poems can be found or are forthcoming in *CARVE, LIT, jacket, puppy flowers, Bombay Gin*, and elsewhere. She lives in Brooklyn.

MELISSA KWASNY is the author of two books of poetry, *The Archival Birds* (Bear Star Press 2000) and *Thistle* (Lost Horse Press 2006, Winner of the Idaho Prize), as well as the editor of *Toward the Open Field: Poets on the Art of Poetry 1800-1950* (Wesleyan University Press 2004). She lives in southwestern Montana.

JOSEPH LEASE's books of poetry include *Broken World* (Coffee House Press, 2007) and *Human Rights* (Zoland, reissued by Jensen/Daniels). His poem "Broken World' (For James Assatly)" was selected for *The Best American Poetry 2002* (Scribner). Lease's poems have also been featured on NPR and published in *The AGNI 30th Anniversary Poetry Anthology, Bay Poetics, Colorado Review, Five Fingers Review, New American Writing, Paris Review, Xantippe*, and elsewhere. Thomas Fink's book *A Different Sense of Power* (Associated University Presses) includes extensive analysis of Lease's poetry. Lease is Chair of the MFA Program in Writing at California College of the Arts.

COLLEEN LOOKINGBILL is co-editor of Etherdome Press with Elizabeth Robinson. Recent poems published or soon to be published in *Switchback, New American Writing, Field and Stream*, and *Xantippe*. Still living in San Francisco's Haight/Ashbury district in a condo building built over the site of a razed Russian rooming house, which back in the '60s held rehearsal/jamming space for Big Brother and the Holding Company and diva of Haight Street, Janis Joplin.

LAURA MORIARTY's most recent books are *Ultravioleta*, a novel, from Atelos *and Self-Destruction*, a book of poetry, from Post-Apollo Press. *A Selected Poetry* is forthcoming from Omnidawn in 2007. She has taught at Mills College and Naropa University, among other places, and is currently Deputy Director of Small Press Distribution. She has two blogs, A Tonalist Notes and Ultravioleta Docs, a continuation of the novel.

TOM ORANGE is a Lecturer in the Department of English and a Learning Specialist in the Disability Support Services office at The George Washington University. He edits the online anthologies at dcpoetry.com and has recent work in *88: A Journal of Contemporary American Poetry, Court Green, Primary Writing* and *PEEKreview.*

JULIET PATTERSON's first book, *The Truant Lover*, was selected by Jean Valentine as the 2004 winner of the Nightboat Poetry Prize and was recently published by Nightboat Books. Poems have appeared in *American Letters &, Commentary, Bellingham Review, New Orleans Review, Washington Square, Verse* and other magazines. She lives near the west bank of the Mississippi in Minneapolis.

BETTINA ROTENBERG received a doctorate from UC Berkeley in Comparative Literature, and now works as the founding director of a non profit called Visual Arts/Language Arts, that sends visual and performing artists and writers into public schools in Richmond and Oakland from preschool through high school. She also teaches poetry to fourth graders in two schools in Richmond as well. She has work in *Millennium Film Journal,Antenym 10, Apex of the M, Sulfur, Dark Ages Clasp the Daisy Root, Screens* and *Tasted Parallels,The Walrus,* and *Natural Bridge.*

EDWARD SMALLFIELD's poems have appeared in *Five Fingers Review, New American Writing, Parthenon West Review, Traverse,26,* and other magazines. He is the author of *The Pleasures of C* and the coauthor *One Hundred Famous View of Edo,* a book length collaboration with Doug MacPherson.

ABDELKRIM TABAL (b.1931), one of Morocco's most honored living poets, is associated with Chefchaouen, the city of his birth. He has said that he composes his poems during his long walks through the maze of narrow, climbing streets whose abrupt turnings and sudden surprises are reflected in his work. Tabal took a degree in Islamic Studies at the Qarawiyin University in Fez, then went on to Tetuan, at that time the cultural capital of Morocco, and published his first poems there. He returned to live in Chefchaouen, where he held the post of Inspector of Arabic Language Education. His own poetic work positions itself in the tradition of modern Arabic poetic practice. He is the recipient of numerous prizes, including Le Prix du Maroc du Livre (1993) for Abir Sabil. His complete works were published under the auspices of the Moroccan Ministry of Culture in 2000. His poems have never before been translated into English.

GAUTAM VERMA has poems out in *Word For/Word, Blaze Vox, Big Bridge, Drunken Boat, Diagram, Moria,* and *PomPom Press* among others, and a trio of chapbooks: *Tombs* and *In Ladakh* from Shearsman, and *Soundings* from Blaze Vox ebooks. He lives and works in Piacenza, Italy.

STEPHEN VINCENT is the recent author of two ebooks, *Triggers* (Shearsman Books, 2005) and *Sleeping with Sappho* (faux Press, 2004), and the forthcoming book, *Walking Theory* (Junction Press, April, 2007). His blog of texts & photographs, critical commentary and politics resides at http://stephenvincent.net/blog/. A longtime editorial presence, he was the director of Momo's Press and Bedford Arts, Publishers and most recently edited *Exploring The Bancroft Library: The Centennial Guide to Its Extraordinary History, Spectacular Special Collections, Research Pleasures, Its Amazing Future and How It All Works* (Bancroft Library/Signature Books). Currently he leads a poetry workshop at the Fromm Institute (USF) and independent 'walking and writing' workshops in the City.

ANNE WALDMAN is an internationally known poet, performer, professor, editor, with strong personal links to the New York School, the Beat Literary Movement, and the experimental strands of the New American Poetry. She has also extended performance to new dimensions with her "modal structures" as in the celebrated "Pieces of An Hour" (for John Cage). She is a Distinguished Professor of Poetics at The Jack Kerouac School of Disembodied Poetics at the Naropa University in Boulder, Colorado, a program she co-founded with poet Allen Ginsberg in 1974. She is the author of over 30 books including, most recently, *Vow To Poetry: Essays, Interviews & Manifestos* (Coffee House Press, 2001), *Marriage: A Sentence* (Penguin Poets, 2000), the twentieth anniversary edition of *Fast Speaking Woman* (City Lights Books), *Iovis: All Is Full of Jove: Books I & II* (Coffee House Press), *Kill or Cure* (Penguin Poets).

WENDY WALKER (www.wendywalker.com) is the author of a novel and two volumes of tales (Sun and Moon Press), numerous critical fictions and *Blue Fire*, an ideogrammatic history of Constance Kent and "the great crime of 1860." *Knots, Selected Tales* edited by L. Timmel Duchamp, was recently published by Aqueduct Press. Her translation (with Rabia Zbakh) of

Abdelkrim Tabal's *Distant Flames* was produced as an artist's book by Florence Neal, and shown at the Proteus Gowanus Gallery/Reading Room in Brooklyn, the Center For Book Arts in Manhattan and at Le Trait Association Committee in Paris.

DEVON WOOTTEN got his MFA from the University of Montana. He is currently in Denmark on a Fulbright Fellowship where he is translating the poems of the Danish poet Sophus Clauseen. He considers himself a reasonably good badminton player.

RABIA ZBAKH holds a degree in English Literature from the University of Abdelmalek Saadi in Tetuan, Morocco. From 1998 to 2002 she coordinated projects of socio-economic development in the province of Chefchaouen. Since 2003 she has worked for the Movimiento por la Paz, el Desarme y la Libertad in Malaga, Spain on projects relating to Morocco.